NEWCOMER
TO THE HORSE WORLD

How to Do Right by Horses …
and Not Be Taken for a Ride

Andrea Sinner, Esq

FOUR
IN HAND
PRESS

First published in 2024
by Four-In-Hand Press
an Imprint of Trafalgar Square Books
North Pomfret, Vermont 05053

Disclaimer of Liability
The author and publisher shall have neither liability nor responsibility to any person or entity with respect to any loss or damage caused or alleged to be caused directly or indirectly by the information contained in this book. While the book is as accurate as the author can make it, there may be errors, omissions, and inaccuracies.

The techniques, ideas, and suggestions in this book are not intended as a substitute for legal, veterinary, or medical advice.

Trafalgar Square Books certifies that the content in this book was generated by a human expert on the subject, and the content was edited, fact-checked, and proofread by human publishing specialists with a lifetime of equestrian knowledge. TSB does not publish books generated by artificial intelligence (AI).

Trafalgar Square Books encourages the use of approved safety helmets in all equestrian sports and activities.

ISBN: 978-1-64601-261-9
Library of Congress Control Number: 2024912892

Cover photo by Helmut Koller
Interior illustration: AdobeStock
Cover design by RM Didier
Interior design by Lauryl Eddlemon
Index by Andrea Jones (JonesLiteraryServices.com)
Typefaces: Minion, Myriad

Printed in the United States of America

10 9 8 7 6 5 4 3 2 1

I dedicate this book to:

1. All the horses I've met … you are perfect and have taught me so much.
2. All the horses I haven't met … you are also perfect.
3. All the horse people who have helped me become a better horsewoman.
4. All the horse people anywhere who work hard every day to do right by horses.
5. All the people who don't consider themselves horse people, yet show love and patience to those of us who are (a bit crazy about horses).
6. You, the reader, for caring enough about the current (or future!) horses in your life to read this book.

And I offer this invitation:

This is the first edition of a book that may or may not find its way into becoming future editions. With that caveat, if anything strikes you as missing or needing to be changed, I welcome your well-contemplated feedback, stories, and pictures.

I promise to review what you send thoughtfully. Should new editions begin to take form, I will use the collective input to expand the value this book offers people and, by proxy, horses. In the meantime, I shall be grateful for what you send, knowing it will enhance my perspective, knowledge, and, importantly, my ability to be a good partner and advocate for the horses in my life.

Please visit my website and click "Book Feedback" (AndreaSinner.com). Before you hit "Submit," please imagine you are sending it to your best friend … that is, please make it truthful (even if it is a hard truth), constructive, and kind.

Contents

Chapter One

The Joy of Being in the Horse World, When You Have a Roadmap

A Pony Named Zingo

A small black pony named Zingo inspired my lifelong passion for horses. My family did not have the desire or the means to introduce me to a life with horses. However, family friends in Woodstock, Vermont, had horses on their property and were avid equestrians. With their support, I attended two weeks of summer camp with Zingo at the Green Mountain Horse Association when I was ten and eleven. I loved every bit of those weeks, and the joy in my face shines in the decades-old pictures I still have.

Living Without Horses for Many Years

Then we moved away from Vermont, which was it—no more real horses for the ensuing decades (though my Breyer* horse collection was impressive). I went to high school and college and embarked on a consulting career where I worked for the next twenty-four years. While traveling the world for work (15 countries),

---

* For those of you unfamiliar with the Breyer horse models, a quick internet search will bring to life this wonderful source of horse beauty since the 1950s.

I started to make enough money that horses were a possibility. When I turned thirty, my best friend and I decided to make our first-ever New Year's resolutions. Mine included finding a hobby to counterbalance my 24/7 work focus. The memory of Zingo (who had long since passed) reminded me that horses could be a magical choice.

Since starting with one lesson a week at a barn that taught both English and Western near where I worked on an out-of-town project in Texas, I have never looked back. Horses became even more important to me as I retired from consulting, attended law school (I was 50 when I got my JD and passed the bar), and started a new career. And so here I am, 25 years into my proper journey with horses, sharing lessons that I hope will help you and, if applicable, your child have more fun and, by proxy, help the horses in your life.

The Danger of Not Knowing What You Don't Know

This is the first lesson of this book. Being a clever pony—they often are—Zingo escaped from his stall one day and wandered his cute self into the feed room. I saw him munching away at a bin with the lid knocked off. I thought, "Well, I guess he's helping himself to an early lunch," and left him to it. Luckily, a few minutes later, I saw the daughter of the family I was visiting (and my idol, given her horse talents), and, luckily again, I thought to mention Zingo's self-served early lunch.

I had never seen a person jump up and run that quickly. I jogged behind her towards the barn, trying to understand the big deal. After she had Zingo back in his stall, she patiently and kindly explained how these majestic and powerful creatures are, in fact, highly delicate in many ways. A horse binging on sweet feed—of course, that was the bin Zingo had selected—can lead to several health issues, all of which are potentially life-threatening. Whether she used words like "colic," "laminitis," or "founder," I do not recall. I was immensely grateful that Zingo had no health issues from that day's events. Upon starting up with horses again, I made it a point to understand the protocols for consistent and constructive feeding patterns.

When you are new, your barn should have feed taken care of, but here are some basics:

- Make sure the feed room doors are securely latched.
- Feed only reasonable amounts.
- When changing types of feed, shift slowly over days or even weeks.
- Include plenty of forage (hay, grass, etc.) in their daily intake.
- Do not feed any horse that is not yours without permission.
- Do not believe all the advertisements for feed and supplements you will see as you delve into the horse world, including those on social media.
- Engage a nutrition expert, preferably brand-independent, if needed.

For the Love of Horses

I spend much of this book giving you the tools to understand what you are getting into when you embark on this journey. If you comprehend the full range of time, energy, passion, and monetary costs, you can make informed decisions and better enjoy the ride.

Before we get into those pesky details, it is worth reflecting on what it could feel like to have horses in your life—whatever variation of a life with horses works for you. Some of you bought this book already understanding why you want horses in your life, and you simply want help being more comfortable and confident in the complex horse world. For those of you who aren't quite sure, especially parents of a horse-mad child, I will try to share what being with horses does for your soul, body, mental health, and connection to the universe. All my fancy words below are an attempt to communicate the feeling you have when a horse:

- Looks upon you and into you with grace and love.
- Permits you in their space when they are at their most vulnerable.
- Gives you 10 times the effort you feel you deserve.
- Teaches you how to be a better human.

Horses Feed Your Soul

Who we are, how we connect to the world around us, how we relate to other beings, and how we expand our consciousness are all fundamental questions of life. I will not argue that all horse people are more evolved than non-horse people, but it is tempting. What I will assert is that when you are with horses, when they see you, when they respond to your energy, when they share their energy, when you learn together, when they make you weep if you do something extraordinary together, and when you are caring for them when they are not well, that teaches your soul.

Horses Develop Your Body

Being with and riding a horse requires being aware of and connected with your body and theirs. At certain levels of riding, you need a unique level of balance, fitness, and further connectedness you would never otherwise develop—every part of your body, mind, energy, and breath matters. The equestrian sports at the Olympics are the only ones without participation requirements related to gender or many patterns related to age. That riding level requires exceptional skills and talent (and money, more on that later), but it is open to women and men, from teenagers to equestrians in their sixties.

Horses Heal Your Mental Health

For many years, I could only ride on weekends (a type of rider commonly referred to as a "weekend warrior"). And yet, even with limited time, I always said that my time with horses was my therapy. My mind stays very busy at all times. That characteristic is an advantage in the professional world but unhelpful when attempting to slow down and take care of yourself. When riding, I cannot think about anything else. Even when simply being at the barn, I remain similarly focused only on horses and all that surrounds them. Innumerable times, horses gave me the reprieve I needed from the stress of work or regular life. I could connect with these fantastic creatures rather than worrying about whatever problems were on that day's list of top stressors.

Horses Connect You to the Universe

This point intertwines with horses feeding your soul. Through horses, in my humble experience, you can feel the presence of the divine. Regardless of your religious or spiritual beliefs, trust that whatever you believe in terms of a higher power will feel stronger through your connection to horses.

What You Can Expect from This Book

If you didn't ride as a child, this book is for you. If it's just been a long time since you have ridden or been around horses, this book is also for you. If your child is enchanted with this sport, and you're not quite sure why and perhaps are worried you could possibly be taken for a ride by the professionals helping your kid, this book is also for you. It is an extraordinary journey to be in the presence of these majestic creatures, and I hope this book helps.

How to Do Right by Horses...and Not Be Taken for a Ride

The core theme of this book is how to "do right" by horses. The simplest way to think about how I use this term is to consider it slang for continually operating with the "best interest of the horse" in mind. For those of you familiar with the term "best interest of the child," you know that it is a holistic and moral framework that guides legal decisions affecting children. Without reaching the level of legalese, what you will find in this book are principles to keep in mind on the many vital topics needed to guide you as you progress in your involvement in the horse world.

Throughout this book I strive to explain that most people in the horse industry care deeply about horses, work harder than most of us every day, and often are barely making ends meet. With that, which should be acknowledged and remembered, another theme of this book is how not to be "taken for a ride" by the less savory characters in the horse world. And so, I also highlight the unfortunate things that can happen to even the smartest of us and how best to avoid those situations.

There is also a twist to the "taken for a ride" theme. I offer many suggestions in this book to help you understand how not to (unwittingly) take others (mainly the horse professionals in your life) for a ride. That is, how to generally be a good client, barn member, show or competition participant, and overall human in this beautiful horse world. There are many cases of amateurs and parents of amateurs behaving badly, and I hope to help you not join their ranks.

Demystifying the Horse World

The horse world generally runs on the apprentice model. It has few accessible (meaning easy to digest rather than overwhelming) documented rules, processes, and guidelines for those new to the sport. When you start in the horse world, it seems like everyone else has been here their whole lives, and you will never catch up. It can even sometimes feel like the insiders are hiding the proverbial ball. And when you've been in the horse world for a while, you will likely be exposed to baffling business, coaching, and animal care practices.

I explain the culture, traditions, conventions, and unwritten rules in this book. I help you ask good questions and second-guess when you get an answer that doesn't feel right. I help you trust your gut, advocate for yourself (and your child if that applies), and be a good advocate for and partner to your horse. And throughout this book, I point you to places where you can find more information. I dream that more people who love horses can more quickly find joy in a way that fits their circumstances. I envision a more welcoming and diverse horse world.

Look to Other Sources to Learn about Horse Care and Riding

You should also know what you will not find in this book. This is not a book about how to ride or a detailed account of how, specifically, to better your horsemanship. There are many brilliant books, articles, blogs, and live events on those topics by people far more knowledgeable than me (note many books are included in the Resources section starting on page 260, and the others are listed on the

"Resources" page of my website, www.AndreaSinner.com). What I provide is a framework for finding a barn, trainer, and horse, and how to make the most of those relationships to improve your riding, horsemanship, and connection with horses and all the wonderful people in the horse world.

The Table of Contents Can Also Guide Online Searches

One of the best parts of this book is the overall structure, and the detailed table of contents and index. You do not need to read everything, but you should read through the table of contents multiple times. It is organized chronologically to cover the journey into a life with horses. But you may need something now that shows up in a later chapter. Familiarizing yourself with the table of contents will help in those scenarios.

The table of contents will also help you find more information online. You can start with the chapter and section titles, and perhaps specific terms or quotes from the book. Then consider adding your chosen discipline, geography, and other relevant details for a search customized to you. If you have learned the magic of generative AI, you know that a well-crafted prompt can produce hugely helpful results. To stay safe, since there remain challenges with AI making up things, make sure to also ask for references and key articles to read. After reading what AI produces, you can then go to the reference articles to both verify the output and understand more context.

Please Know—Even I Don't Always Follow My Own Advice

This book is filled with countless bits of advice. Much comes from my personal experience making mistakes and finding a better way; the rest comes from watching and learning from others. And yet, for all that solid counsel, unless it is related to health and safety, I don't always follow my own advice. Sometimes I forget or let myself get distracted, and sometimes I just can't be bothered. Pick the recommendations that sound like a good fit for you and try them out. For each bit that works, try to stick with it. And when you "know better" and still make a mistake (you will, as we all do), be gentle with yourself, figure out what you learned from it, and commit to doing better next time.

A final introductory note: throughout this book, horses are generally referred to using male pronouns. I love girl horses, too (as evidenced by my perfect chestnut mare, Gigi, who is on the cover of this book), but for clarity and ease of reading, I have chosen a "default" to use instead of alternating.

Chapter Two

Start with Intention, and Enjoy the Ride

I'm Here for a Break from My Stressful Career

A few years into my riding and one year into owning my first horse, I had to find a new barn when moving to a new city. Through my research, I ended up at a large barn with a nice balance of adults and juniors. Though I could only ride on the weekends, I enjoyed my horse and the mental health tune-ups that being around horses always gave me. I was even up for going to the occasional show. Mainly, though, I wanted to improve my riding and have a wonderful distraction from the intensity of being a newly promoted partner in a global consulting firm. I had set my intentions, found the right place for me and my horse, and enjoyed everything.

Then, one day in a lesson, a trainer disrupted my happy equilibrium. They screamed at me that I wasn't trying hard enough during an exercise I could not get right. It was one of those moments when you expect to hear the screech of a needle on a record coming to a halt (yes, an old-fashioned vinyl record). Really? In the next moment, I responded at a similar volume—with the addition of profanity—that I was trying as hard as I could. Then, in a quieter conversation not overheard by everyone in the barn as those outbursts had been, I shared why that coaching style was unacceptable to me. I chose riding to be with horses and horsepeople. I was keen to improve my riding and my horsemanship. But I wanted it to be fun and serve as my respite from the corporate world. I had never had a client or colleague scream at me; enduring that from someone I was paying was outrageous. We had a productive conversation and reset our relationship; they never yelled at me again, and I never swore loudly in anger again.

I share this somewhat humorous and somewhat terrible story for two reasons. First, you have a right to hold your ground in whatever way required so your horse experience stays aligned with your values (for me, a top value was having a pleasurable break from the intensity of my career). Second, unless there is an imminent safety issue for a horse or a human, screaming—the angry and aggressive kind—in a lesson is unacceptable. It is unpleasant, unprofessional, and almost exclusively unproductive.

You Have More Control of This Journey Than You Might Think

When new in the horse world, most of us happen upon a barn and a trainer and then follow their program. We might share with them our monthly budget and then do as we are told. That describes how I initially operated decades ago. This book is dedicated to helping you be more disciplined and purposeful every step of the way, including finding your first barn, so you feel comfortable and confident faster than those of us who bumbled along in the early days.

This chapter explains how to clarify your objectives, collaborate respectfully with a professional to create a reasonable plan, start the journey, keep it productive and fun, and evolve your strategy as needed. The more time you spend on self-reflection to clarify why you are starting a life with horses, the better it will feel. When you understand your core values, you have the power to make productive choices. Horse professionals generally have to intuit what you're looking for, partly because most new riders (and their parents) don't know enough to communicate well. After reading this chapter and working through the exercises, you and your trainer will be well set up for a successful collaborative partnership.

Know That You Belong

Envision the Great Joy of Being with Horses—It's Why You're Here

I love animals. I love people, too, but animals speak to me differently. When I was writing this book, a horse friend reflected that I might scare you away in my effort to help you go into the horse world with eyes wide open. The daunting time, energy, emotional, and financial commitments should be considered when seeking all that a love of horses brings. I discussed the joy horses bring in the section on page 3, describing how horses feed your soul, body, mental health, and connection to the universe; let me dig down a layer here.

Life is a journey. Horses are a journey. The joy comes from all of it, not just the good parts. If you tire of the message that adversity builds strength and resilience, you might want to skip ahead. The hard times are not "joyous" in the moment, yet they plant the seeds for "joy" in the future. Through a change in perspective or the development of a newly necessitated skill, something grows in you when you are present for every moment. The goal is not to stress over that last jump or barrel or leg yield (or whatever it is in your horse discipline) or have anxiety about the next one, but to be fully present in the moment, learning and trying to do better.

The Goodness That Is Horses…There Are No Bad Horses

Let's start with the good parts. Horses have a beautiful way of getting under your skin. They see you for who you are. They will stand with you when you need a good cry. They are the masters of setting reasonable boundaries and will let you know when you don't get it right. They won't let you lie to them or yourself. They have noses that are silky, lips that are curious, ears that are indicators, and person-alities that are as complex as our own. When you are slow and patient, you will develop a strong partnership built on mutual respect.

Some horses are more expressive than others, but don't expect them to always treat you like the center of their universe. As you become their person, you will feel some of that. But horses are not like dogs; they do not have the canine "you are the best, and I will follow you everywhere" approach to life. Horses are also not like cats; though horses can be detached, they do not have the feline "you clearly exist to service me" mentality.*

"Welcome Home, Mom!" (Said My Horse, Joplin)

STORY

And now for a story to refute my canine comparison above. After I bought my first horse, Joplin, work necessitated a move to the UK. I left Joplin behind for a bit, not wanting him to make the trip across the pond if the project didn't work out. I found a magnificent farm in north-central Florida with fantastic care, turnouts, and people. They checked in regu-larly during what was basically a non-working sabbatical for him and did all the right things. Upon my first visit back a few weeks into his stay, I entered his heavenly 2-acre paddock and called his name, as he was at the far side. He picked up his head and then galloped in my direction. I stood with open arms as he crossed the field.

Watching a horse run unencumbered by humans is a beautiful thing to see. Watching one run *to you* is breathtaking. He did a small barrel-race-turn around me (his job was jumps rather than barrels, but he got it done) and came in for a nuzzle. That horsey moment goes in the great—not just good, but great—category. Priceless. Especially to me, when I was just a couple of years into a life with horses and was working and traveling 24/7.

---

* Please forgive my dog and cat generalities. I love all dogs and all cats, but their pat-terns do illustrate the point above well.

Any question about whether this whole thing was a good idea evaporated at that moment. There have been so many more such moments, but this one sealed my love for and commitment to my expensive horse addiction.

The House That Machu Built

I don't even know where to start this story. Everything you will read in this book tells you I love all horses. They are perfect, regardless of pedigree or occupation. I have also had a small number of heart horses who were and are life-changing for me.

But this story is about a horse who changed so many lives that it almost defies rational thought. Not that he is the only horse to have had such an impact—there are many, and all their stories should be told—but this is the one horse I have had the privilege to know who truly embodies greatness.

Skara Glen's Machu Picchu (Machu) is now happily retired after his amazing career, and revels in being the king of his new domain of massive Virginia fields. The other geldings in his friendly, relaxed herd, and his human visitors coming to give love and attention, are his subjects. Not that Machu is anything but kindly, but his regal air sets him apart.

Backing up a bit, Machu's prior realm was the world of international showjumping. He competed at the five-star level for eight years and was made for it. I have a video of him walking in the hangar of a European airport after a flight to compete there—his presence and swagger are what you might expect of your favorite rock star.

But what showed in the ring, and underneath that ethereal attitude, was pure heart—he gave every stride and every jump just that bit more energy, focus, and effort than one might believe possible. Showing the heart of a warrior. The heart of a champion.

I was a latecomer to join the brilliant syndicate and rider who supported this beautiful creature for so many years. But I was in time to behold many magnificent jumps, classes, and events, and be part of his daily life. The syndicate members frequently traveled together to bear witness to Machu and his rider doing amazing things—we all felt lucky to be there.

Hundreds of people contribute to top-level events: riders, grooms, coaches, vets, farriers, shippers, bodyworkers, sports psychologists, show staff, owners, and more. For me, knowing that incredible horse, kissing his nose regularly, knowing the strength in his body (via a pat from the ground rather than riding), watching him feed off the crowd (which he believed was there to watch only him), and helping in my small way has been a profound experience.

When Machu was recognized at formal gatherings beyond competitions, I was struck by the number of people he touched, how we all showed up, and our shared struggle to explain just how much he meant to us. If you ever properly met or supported Machu, you were welcomed into a family bound by a commitment to his health, longevity, and success. And all of us are honored to forever live in the house that Machu built.

Challenges in the Horse World...Most Are Human-Generated

It is also essential to consider the horse journey's less-than-good parts. Most of the challenges you will face come from people. This includes other riders, friends and family of other riders, professionals, service providers, and sometimes random strangers with opinions (thank you, social media). There is a term, "barn drama," which refers mainly to unhelpful chatter and gossip. There's the insecure person constantly judging others behind their back, and they can always find someone to listen. The entitled teen looking down upon another junior for not having the right fancy brand of whatever they deem important. Then someone says something about someone else and the gossip machine turns it from inane to hurtful. It does become more serious when it relates to the blame game that happens when someone is hurt, a horse is hurt, and belongings go missing.

Above I bring up social media—where I am a consumer rather than a current contributor—because it can be a very dangerous place, especially if it is your child who is the new rider. We all know most people only show the good stories on their feeds. While social media is a necessary tool for most people in the horse business, much of what is out there is polished, unrealistic fiction. I follow people who actively post the good, the bad, and the ugly, because it is so refreshing; professionals who share real equestrian insights, without it seeming like propaganda; and horse brands and horse photographers because they have the money and talent respectively to post simply stunning horse photos. Note that none of the bad parts of social media are horse-generated!

Some of the challenges you face will come from the horses themselves. Your horse isn't sound, and it's unclear why. Your horse seems determined to hurt himself in turnout. Your horse has developed a behavior that is annoying, or perhaps even scary. Your horse doesn't seem happy in the job you are having him do. For all of this, great joy can come from working on the problem, slowly getting to the answers, and growing your horsemanship skills in the process. Nobody wants problems with their horse, but they are inevitable. Enjoying the journey means facing and loving that reality as well.

Get to Know the Language of the Horse World

Every culture, sport, business, and even family has its own language. The horse world is no different. Some elements of this language are technical (horse body parts, tack names, and more), and others seem more colloquial (lingo for a horse's temperament, description of how a horse moves in certain gaits, and so on). I am still learning terms and find it fascinating when engaging with people from different geographies and disciplines.

Even though I discovered them only recently, I am enamored with the Pony Club manuals (you can find online via www.ponyclub.org), which are as comprehensive as anything you can find online. Additionally, as a starting (and free) resource, Wikipedia is as good as any, especially the page titled "Glossary of Equestrian Terms."

Any list that has "whinny or whinney," says, "see *neigh*," and has additional pages for "equine anatomy," "list of horse breeds," and more is a great place to start.

When you are a newcomer, this is plenty. And though I could refine the list, I really can't add more than the product of what open-source and open-verification offers. In the Resources section starting on page 260, I list other books and reference materials where you can dig further as you better understand what interests you.

Expand Your Relationships with Horse People

Find All the Horse People You Can…and Ask Everyone for Someone Else They Recommend

Horse people have many opinions and stories, and love to talk about horses. Non-horse people (especially partners of horse people) can attest to this as they have undoubtedly been forced to listen to endless conversations about horse care, riding, showing, and barn drama at the dinner table. If you have a friend in the horse world, ask them to take you along when they go out with their horsey friends. If you are starting and don't know anybody, ask one person at every barn you visit (see Chapter 4 about the barn search process starting on page 112) if you could buy them coffee or a glass of wine—these are the two types of fuel on which many humans in the horse world run.

Listen to everyone and ask any question that comes to mind. Even the most seasoned and famous horse people are kind and open with beginners. Indeed, my experience is that the top horse people (professionals, amateurs, vets, grooms, farriers, etc.) are happy to talk with anyone with a genuine and thoughtful interest—as long as they are not about to go in the ring or are busy with a horse or client. As a newcomer, nothing is out of bounds in any of these conversations other than, "How much did you pay for your horse?" (they might offer that information if you are horse shopping, but it's not great to ask). The Barn Evaluation Template starting on page 134 lists questions you might want to ask a potential barn or trainer, but at the end of this subsection are some questions you could ask any horse person over your beverage of choice.

Include People Who Have No Vested Interest in Your Choices

There are two categories of people with whom you will be speaking: those with a vested interest in how you move forward with horses, and those without. I speak here of a financial interest. Those with a vested interest are predominantly prospective trainers, barn owners, and people with horses to sell. A prospective trainer is a fantastic person you can chat with, yet know it is almost impossible for them to be objective (especially if they really like you and would love to have you in their barn).

Those without a vested interest are everyone else. Another adult at a barn or another mom of a rider at a barn might want you to join their barn (because they also think you are super-cool and want you around), but they can be more objective. Horse people who ride somewhere other than where you are considering can be gold; the exception is when they had one bad experience ten years ago with someone and strangely still can't be objective today (long-term grudges happen a lot in the horse world). And remember that anyone involved with horses includes those who work at barns, tack shops, shippers, veterinary offices, and so on. The broader your search, the better your comprehensive knowledge. I have learned more from the grooms—many with decades of experience—than almost any other group of professionals (see page 205 for A Special Note on Grooms).

Some questions you might ask horse people:

- What brought you into a life with horses? And what keeps you here?
- I'm new to all this; what is your advice for me?
- The number of barns to choose from is bewildering. Do you have any experiences or (verified) stories you can share about any of these barns that might be helpful?
- Could you share a story (or many) of a beautiful moment you had with your horse or horses?
- Could you share a story (or many) of when you made a mistake in your early days with horses? What do you wish you had known before that event?
- Is there anyone I should watch out for? Why?

- What are the three best things and worst things about your barn and trainer?
- How engaged are you in caring for your horse, or does the barn staff do most of it?
- How does your business (if they have a company serving the horse world) engage with horses and their humans? What are your best and worst stories from supporting this world?
- What are the worst things a newcomer to the horse world can do, and how do I avoid being that person?

Honor Your Responsibilities to—and the Rights of— Every Horse in Your Sphere

A horse is a being worthy of care. They are creatures of beauty and majesty that deserve our respect for their well-being and interests. You have vital responsibilities when you engage with horses and bring them into your life. Whether you plan to volunteer for a charitable organization that helps children through therapeutic riding or seek to buy a horse and compete at a high level, consider the principles below. I also include here my view of the fundamental rights of horses. Of course, very few of these are legal rights, but they align with the views of the most caring, humane, and dedicated horse people I know.

Before diving into those details, consider doing this 2–3-minute silent practice after you park your car at the barn, where you will encounter horses, before you open your car door:

- Take several deep breaths. **Clear your energy** and mind, and leave behind anything negative you were dealing with before you arrived.
- Take more deep breaths. **Set your intention** for how you will be present and engage with the horses and people in the barn.
- Take a few more deep breaths. **Express your gratitude** for this chance to be with horses and for everything this time together will bring.
- Then, open your car door and **bask in the amazingness of being with horses**.

ENGAGING WITH HORSES

The Horse's Rights

1. To be protected and treated well (at the most basic level, not to be mistreated or subjected to avoidable suffering).

2. To be adequately fed, sheltered, and provided with quality medical and farrier care.

3. To be recognized as his own being—with feelings and quirks, likes and dislikes, strengths and weaknesses, and good days and bad days (yes, just like us).

4. To be in a job that suits his body, character, age, and natural abilities (know that sometimes this implies he is best suited to be a magnificent lawn ornament).

5. To be cared for his entire natural life (my point: retire the horse, when necessary and in adequate circumstances, rather than leave him to a system that often leads to neglect, mistreatment, and slaughter).

Your Responsibilities

1. Find your Zen when you are with horses (breathe, go slow, revel in their majesty, bask in their energy and graciousness).

2. Love them and make sure they know you are their person (whether that be for a moment, a lesson, or a lifetime).

3. Interact with your horse (sharing space, groundwork, aids, training, riding) with positive intent (read: without negative emotion or personal baggage from your day; yet know they can help you heal old and new wounds…allow them to work their magic on you).

4. Find the best care team possible, one that you trust (this applies to horses for whom you are responsible, and includes the barn, trainer, groom, vet, farrier, shipper, and more).

5. Commit to the time, energy, physical, emotional, and financial responsibilities necessary to fulfill the Horse's Rights.

Be Respectful of All the People with Whom You Interact

Regardless of your chosen discipline, you will engage with many people in the horse world. The most important ones are those on your horse care team (explored in Chapter 6—see page 184). Other people include those in your barn, those who run and work at shows (if you decide to show), other riders from different barns (if you choose to show), other horse owners (if you buy or sell a horse), and so on. This sounds trite, but if you are friendly and honest, follow the general protocols of the horse world, fulfill your commitments, and truly stick to your own business, you will do fine.

Though more detail is included in the section starting on page 230, here is a simple list of guidelines for generally good behavior:

- Safety is job one (for horses and people).
- Be good to your horse (see the table on p. 19).
- Be on time (or early).
- Pay your bills on time (or early).
- Ask about prices in advance instead of moaning about the size of the bills after.
- Don't interrupt other conversations (for example, your trainer talking to another client).
- Don't gossip.
- Don't take other people's gossip seriously.
- Be respectful of everyone.
- Say thank you to everyone, especially staff.
- If you commit to something, do it.
- If you can't meet a commitment on time or at all, notify the people depending on you ASAP.
- If you make a mistake (you will!), own it and fix it.
- Clean up after yourself and your horse (aisle, wash stalls, arena).
- Put your stuff away.
- Smile, say hello, laugh, and tell every horse owner their horse is stunning/perfect. Because he is.
- Don't feed other people's horses without permission.
- Don't use other people's stuff without permission.
- Don't comment on another rider's mistake in the ring.
- Pass other riders in a ring in the left-to-left model.
- If someone violates the left-to-left model, avoid a collision anyway.

Be Around Horses for (Close to) Free before You Start Spending $

In the section on page 55, I present various options for how to escalate your involvement with horses. The best way to start is to spend time with the minimal expenditure necessary to be in the presence of horses. This approach applies to both you and your child (no matter how much they beg for their own pony on day one).

Even if you have the means to start spending big, I love the idea of volunteering at a charitable organization first (and yes, your job may be solely to muck stalls or fill water buckets as you are not qualified for much else, and they will even have to teach you how to do that). You can also volunteer at horse shows, audit clinics, and take advantage of online learning opportunities with different riding associations and organizations.

In these early days at a charitable organization or a barn, ask where it is okay to "hang out." Comply with the boundaries you are given. And then sit with it and consider: Do any of the following move you?

- Watching a horse in his paddock.
- Listening to a horse munch on hay or grain.
- Watching a lesson with either newcomers or those with more experience.
- Listening to people at the barn chat about their horses.
- Smelling the barn, horses, tack, grain…all of it.
- Listening to the sound of hoofsteps when a horse walks down the aisle.
- Watching a horse's ears as he interacts with everything around him.

After you have been around horses for a while, if any of this speaks to you and your child, consider progressing your involvement with horses. As an aside, the best horse parents I know are as moved by horses as their children, even if they do not want to ride themselves. I define "best horse parents" as ones who are supportive of, attentive to, and patient with both their child and the horse with whom they entrust their child.

Understand the Myriad of Ways You Can Be with Horses

Most of this book focuses on providing insights for those who eventually want to ride horses within a discipline (more on the concepts of disciplines below). Even if that is what you have in mind, it is essential to remember that there is no single right way to engage with horses. If you are an adult rider, the principles below should be easy to digest and take on board. If you are a parent to a junior rider, these principles remain true and may be hard for your child to comprehend when they think "everyone" engages with horses in a certain way, and they want to be a part of it.

You Can Enjoy the Majesty of Horses without Ever Putting Tack on Them

Those who ride regularly understand they are lucky to simply be around horses. You do not need a halter, saddle, or harness for a horse to teach you about yourself or bring out your inner child. So before you jump into all the fantastic disciplines humans have created as ways to structure and assess their time with horses, start with sharing space.

There Are Many Disciplines in Which You Can Engage

The list of horse disciplines (specialized equestrian activities with unique emphases and rules) is extensive. Wikipedia has a page for "List of Equestrian Sports," and for those of you in the United States, the page for the "United States Equestrian Federation" lists the (large) subset of disciplines within their purview.

If I listed disciplines here, I would no doubt offend some passionate horse people by missing their specific discipline. And I would offend other people by including disciplines that they believe can be abusive to horses (and, in some cases, I would agree with them). Rather than providing such a list, I share questions to ponder as you contemplate how you would like to engage with horses:

- Are there horse facilities near me that treat horses in a way that aligns with my beliefs about how horses should be treated? (If you don't yet have strong beliefs on horse treatment, visit as many horse places as possible…observe, let it wash over you, and see what feels best). If so, which disciplines do they offer? Do I like the people there, in addition to the horses? (An extensive Barn Evaluation Template starts on page 134; this is a simple gut check.)

- What type of bond between horse and human is showcased in the disciplines I find interesting? What is the objective of the endeavor and, if applicable, of the related "sport"?
- In the disciplines I find interesting, am I comfortable with how horses appear to be treated at the…
  » Entry-level (where I will be when I start)?
  » Top-level (from what I can see online or perhaps in person)?
  » End of the human-defined "productive" life of the horse?
  » End of the natural life of the horse?
- What are the time, energy, physical, emotional, and financial requirements expected for this discipline (keeping in mind there is always a massive range of options), and do they match my capabilities and constraints?

Even if you picked up this book with your heart set on reining, dressage, or driving, you might want to adjust based on your early research. Or you may decide to change later.

You Can Change How You Engage with Horses Whenever You Like

After starting up with horses however you choose, you will grow and learn in the ensuing months and years. Remember, however, that there are no rules about sticking with a particular path once you have embarked upon it. It will take time and likely money for new tack and trappings to change—and if you own a horse, it can be much more complicated and you have responsibilities there, but that is all up to you.

Some people adjust based on an injury (horse-related or otherwise) to feel safer. Others shift to a discipline some people consider less safe. And still others decide to refocus on caring for horses and enjoying that time rather than participating in any particular "sport." You are in the early days now, but know that the entire journey remains your call. You have the agency to adjust to what feels most authentic to you, as long as you do right by any horse you are responsible for.

If You Love Horses, Know That You Belong in the Horse World

The horse world can be varying degrees of elusive and exclusive, depending on your chosen discipline and level. And, to finish the alliteration, expensive… horses and horse sports come with significant costs (see Chapter 3 starting on page 47 for details). However, simply being able to spend money does not necessarily mean horses are for you. As a start, consider yourself on the right track toward belonging in the horse world if these two simple things are true:

- You respect the majesty of horses.
- You read the section above on responsibilities and rights (on page 19) and thought, "Yes, to all this!"

STORY

Even When You Get One of the Silly Rules Wrong…
You Still Belong

Early in my involvement with horses and riding, I lived in southern California. It was sweltering for a casual day of riding and nobody else (or so I thought) was around. As I might have done when working out in a gym, I decided that wearing just my (high-coverage) sports bra was a cunning plan. I had a great ride, and my attire was well-suited to the heat. Happy days.

As you might guess, especially given that it was a fancy hunter/jumper barn, I was "talked to" about my inappropriate attire. It was not a scolding, more of a "please don't do that again." Though I remember it well, I do not remember being embarrassed or too concerned about the whole thing. I was practical, they were silly, and yet, in the future, I would comply with these now-known rules.

Many horse people reading this will scoff at this story as silly ("In my part of the horse world, we wear what we like!" I can hear them say), and they are not wrong. Yet, from all my conversations with horse people, every discipline has a few hidden rules that defy logic.

I put that story here as it demonstrates that even when I was unwittingly audacious and operating outside the norms of that barn, it had no bearing on whether I belonged in the horse world. I had done all the important things right—slowly warming up my horse, not working him too hard in the heat, spending time for a proper cooldown, hosing him down, and letting him dry while munching grass in the shade. If the discipline I had chosen at that time (as mentioned above, others would not care) was testy about a bare midriff, then okay. I adjusted by finding cooler tops to wear on hot days and moved on with my horsey life. And today, over twenty years later, I long for the days when I would consider showing my belly in public in the first place.

Commitment to Animal Welfare Matters...
Which Brands You Wear Do Not

At its worst, some will judge you more for the trappings of the sport than for your commitment to animal welfare. There are critiques of brands of gear (when only function matters), fanciness of a stable and farm (when only cleanliness, organization, and safety for the horses and riders matter), performance in a single class or show (when it's the longevity of the horse in a lifestyle suited to him that matters), and whether your hairnet, socks, or helmet are "right" (being well turned-out is a fine objective, but should not be overplayed to the point of ridiculousness).

Ignore all this noise to the degree possible. Peer pressure is hard, especially for children and juniors, but 95 percent of the sources of pressure, like these examples, are daft (I love this informal British word, "daft," which generally means, "silly, foolish, mad, insane.") Let it go and stand proud in doing the right thing for you, your child if applicable, and your horse (not with the pompous view you know the "only" way, but proud of doing it your own great way).

You Belong More than Any "Seasoned" Person
Who Does Terrible Things to Horses

When money, prestige, and ego drive decisions, even human athletes can suffer mistreatment. The risk is higher for horses. Many people view horses as simply a means to their ends, not as sensitive creatures worthy of good treatment.

Note: The following paragraph and list are hard to read. You should read them, but if you're relaxing in bed and these are the last things you'll read before you sleep...read them tomorrow.

Though people in the horse world will not be surprised, you might be. Here it is: there are people at every level of every equestrian sport who do bad things to horses. Sometimes, these actions come from ignorance, while other times, they are intentional. Regardless of the reason, horses pay the price for these abhorrent human behaviors. The list is longer than I share here, but even this brief tour of bad things is a hard list to face:

- Neglect (insufficient food and water; unsanitary and cramped living conditions; inadequate veterinary and farrier care; allowing to become overweight).
- Abuse (beating or otherwise harming with and without implements/weapons; over-working/training; over-injecting/medicating—aka, drugging).
- Discarding once not "useful" to humans (slaughter versus retirement; a bad "retirement" leading to neglect, death, and slaughter).
- Death/murder for the insurance money.

Know it is possible, loathe it, call it out when you see it, and vow to be a better human than those people.

You Know You Belong When...

Leaving that unsavory topic behind, let's return to you with your good soul who wants to do right by horses. In addition to the factors at the beginning of this section, my view is that table stakes for belonging in the horse world are:

- You intend to do right by these equine athletes.
- You commit to doing better when you make a mistake and do something (by action or inaction) not in line with that intention.
- You commit to extending your involvement with horses only as far as you can back up that intention.

If you half-lease a horse and care for him well (in line with the responsibilities and rights listed above), then you belong as much as any rider with five fancy horses who is taking home multiple blue ribbons at a top-rated show. Suppose you volunteer at a horse rescue or therapeutic riding center and remind every horse how perfect they are every day you are there to help. In that scenario, you belong as much as anyone at the top end of their chosen sport (and trust me, the good people at that level are very grateful for your kind efforts). And in either of those scenarios, you belong more than those who treat horses predominantly as servants to their egos and bank accounts with little to no regard for the animals' long-term welfare.

You belong when you know that horses are the end, not the means, full stop (sharing space and energy with horses is the goal, even if you are striving toward a competitive objective). Quite simply, even in your earliest days with horses, you belong more than those who believe horses are a means to some other self-serving end. The decisions you make every day will demonstrate your commitment to prioritizing the welfare of horses over time.

Be a Good Advocate for Yourself

Regardless of Your Age When You Start, Riding Requires a Level of Fitness

Walking around almost any barn or horse show, you will notice a wide range of ages (read: everyone is welcome!). Depending on your geography and horse discipline, there may be a disparity in gender representation, but it is generally inclusive, if sometimes imbalanced, especially at the higher levels. When it comes to body type, most can be effective riders. You might think only modestly tall and super thin people can make it in this sport (there are many of them, so this preconceived notion is reasonable). Tall people do have an advantage in the early days of riding, as it is easier for us to "wrap our legs around" a horse when trying not to fall off. But skill, fitness, and balance matter far more than height. Indeed, there are very famous five-foot-nothing riders with more grit and riding capability in their small stature than most of us could ever dream of.

Capability Matters More than Weight…but Weight Does Matter

The biomechanics of the combination of horse, discipline, and rider should govern the boundaries for weight. Recently, there has been some contention regarding the weight of riders. An unskilled and heavy rider can negatively impact how a horse feels in his body. A similarly heavy person who is a talented rider on an appropriately sized horse has a better chance of forming a suitable pairing.

There are a great many people in the horse world who might be described as underweight for what is healthy for a person of their age, height, and body type. Not only is that their business generally, but in riding, being at that end of the weight spectrum does not present risks to horses. Conversely, it is only logical that there is a weight limit beyond which it is unreasonable to expect a horse to bear a rider on his back. Be reasonable and put the welfare of the horse first. There are many articles and guidelines on this topic…I suggest you go to those. And please remember, this is not about shaming any body type; it's about physics and the biomechanics of horses. That's as far as I'll dip my toe into this contentious water.

Being Fit Makes the Process More Fun and Progress Easier

One thing that can hold you back in your riding and horsemanship is not having a basic fitness level. Children adapt quicker, but parents reading this should know that the rule still applies to them. You will reap the benefits if you make a modest effort to be in reasonable shape—you do not need to be a star athlete, just able to access a certain amount of muscular, coordination, and aerobic capacity. Though you will use specific muscles when riding that can't be worked any way other than riding, you have many areas of fitness you can develop.

- **Core strength**: This is fundamental. However you work on it (my favorite is Pilates), having a strong core will help you ride and work around horses (grooming, lifting, laughing, and more).
- **Balance and flexibility**: Every rider has imbalances in body structure, flexibility, and fitness. This can lead to inconsistency in the aids you use with your horse, generating an imbalance in your horse. Given that the horse also has his own natural imbalances (that you will try to help him with), your being as even and balanced as possible will help him.
- **Endurance**: Depending on your riding objectives, you may need to improve your aerobic capacity. When you're having a great ride or trying to fix something with your horse during a ride, it is unhelpful to have to stop for more breaks than your horse needs (I know this to be true, as I am a master at taking breaks and realize I should be able to take fewer of them).

A special note for the older reader: Take all of this advice regarding fitness even more seriously. You likely already are if you're considering having horses, but it is worthy of focus. I used to ski one week a year. The first time I was properly fit for that one week, I was stunned by how much more "talented" I was at skiing. It was, of course, fitness rather than talent. Horseback riding is the same. Even periodic efforts aligned with the points above will pay dividends in your riding.

Understand This Is a Dangerous Sport—Be Safe and Be Prepared
Examples of a Horse Inadvertently Hurting His Human

Horses are giant creatures who do unpredictable things. Whether you are around or on them, you must always have safety for them and you in mind. They do not have bad intentions (though sometimes bite and kick as a defensive or protective action) and yet can wreak havoc with seemingly no effort.

- A horse standing on the crossties, spooked by someone nearby making a sudden movement? He may inadvertently step on your foot.
- A horse annoyed by flies around his front legs? He may quickly bend a knee when you're in the wrong position brushing his legs, and knock you in the head (yes, this has happened to me...and yes, this happened to someone else I know, and she was knocked out cold).
- You decided to ride for that one short trail ride without a helmet? That will be when a deer jumps into the path, and you suddenly fall and hit your head.
- A cute horse you don't know sticking his cute head out of the stall, seemingly to say hello? Someone failed to put a sign noting he is a biter, and now you have teeth marks to prove it.
- Think half a glass of wine can't possibly slow your reaction time enough to be dangerous for a ride? Quite simply, don't test this one. Alcohol impairs reaction time and judgment...both are vital when you are around horses, let alone riding one. If you see others drinking and riding, do not succumb to peer pressure, and make sure you and your horse are safely away from the antics. If you are a parent and see others drinking and riding in front of your kid, tell your trainer that it is unacceptable, give them a chance to

adjust, and if you are not happy with the behavioral response, you might consider changing barns.

Examples of a Horse Saving His Human from Potential Harm

You should also know that horses don't always cause problems. Horses can and do frequently make heroic efforts to save you from yourself.

- Fall off your horse and somehow end up next to him rather than under him? Many horses have contorted themselves and seemingly levitated mid-stride or mid-jump to avoid stepping on, landing on, or hurting their person.
- Leave the stall door open by accident, and your horse lets himself out? Though this could end badly, he will often hunt down the closest person or spot with food and happily be returned to his stall (bring a food bribe with you, or he may not believe you next time).
- Lost your seat a bit at the first jump of a one-stride combination? It is not uncommon for a horse to jump the next one in a way that helps you get fully back in the saddle. It sounds impossible, yet I have had multiple horses do that for me.

Your trainer will work with you to ensure you have the appropriate safety gear and that it fits you, but here is a short list:
- Certified helmet.
- Footgear with a proper heel.
- Safety vest.

Safety equipment takeaways:
- **Make sure your helmet fits.** This is an item you need to buy in person, or else you must be really sure of your size—perhaps with help from your barn—if you need to buy online. A good salesperson at your local tack shop can help you through the process of finding something that feels a bit

too tight and yet is probably right. Your barn will hopefully have you try on a bunch they have around to see what might work. Keep in mind that if you are trying on old helmets at your barn, the padding might be compressed and styles might have changed, so what you order online may not fit correctly when you receive it. Whether you buy your helmet in a shop or online, leave the tags on until you have confirmation from your trainer that you have found a good fit.

- **Get the latest helmet technology.** Horse people have suffered every injury you can imagine. Wearing a helmet is vital. It may not save you, but the statistics demonstrate you will fare better. The newest technology is designed to reduce the frequency and severity of concussions.

- **Take any hit to the head seriously.** The sports world is learning more and more about the effects of repeated hits to the head and concussions. Though horseback riding does not mean taking regular impacts to the head, even periodic falls with a blow to a helmet-protected head can still result in concussions. I have been there and was in the ICU for two days as a result.

- **Replace your helmet after a fall, or every five years.** Most people don't know or forget to tell you that you should buy a new helmet if you fall and hit your helmet-covered head. That few-hundred-dollar item you bought two months ago? Yup, throw it away and buy another. I know they're expensive, but once they've taken a hit, a visual inspection might not tell you that the protective nature of the helmet was compromised by the impact. This is not a rule made up by helmet manufacturers to make more money; according to the research and articles I have found, it is a legitimate rule to follow.

- **Wear the safety vest—all the cool people do.** This is a discipline-specific comment (in some disciplines, this is entirely foreign), but I think everyone should wear a safety vest. Even when you and your horse are in good form, things happen. Eventers have been wearing body protector vests for years. With the advent of comfortable, effective air vests, more riders in more disciplines are wearing them. I love seeing the top show jumpers wear them; they set an excellent example for everyone competing in that discipline.

Again...Please Take Any Hit to the Head Seriously

STORY

Fifteen years into my riding career, I was casually walking on my super-safe horse, Guinness, along a path at a massive horse show when he noticed there was a hot walker (a giant contraption that goes in circles to walk horses) on the other side of the hedge. We had passed this hot walker many times, but it was moving this time, and that difference made it a horse-eating monster. Guinness spun 180 degrees, and off I came. I landed on my back and hit my helmet-covered head. I felt good after dusting myself off, so I hand-walked Guinness the rest of the way to the ring to re-mount and take my lesson. Horse people rightly want to know if Guinness ran away after he spooked, thus having to be caught and brought back to me. Nope; after his pirouette, he just stood there looking down at me (a blessing, as we were nowhere near our stalls, any of the rings, or any other humans).

Two weeks later, I was periodically, and uncharacteristically so, irritable and forgetful. I connected the dots and went to the student health center (even though I was 47 at the time, I was a student at the law school and thus was part of the university's health system). At universities with big football programs, they know a lot about concussions. They immediately performed all the requisite tests, including a CT scan. The results were thankfully encouraging. Yes, a mild concussion. But no, there was nothing special to do other than avoid hitting my head again.

Five years later—you can guess where this is going—I fell while riding and hit my helmet-covered head again (yes, it was a new helmet since the last time). I had been taking a jumping lesson, and everything was going fabulously well. And then, at a modest jump, I came off. Everyone watching waited for me to pop back up; by all accounts, it just didn't look like a nasty fall. Gigi, my horse, had levitated and contorted herself to not step on me and didn't run away. (Anyone who knows me is waiting for me to say this somewhere in this book, so I will put it here: All. My. Horses. Are. Perfect.)

For my part, I threw up in the ambulance, was in the ICU for two days, and still don't remember about three hours of that day. I spent months in recovery from vertigo, nausea, and a failing memory. I didn't ride for six months. I would say it was a full year before I felt normal again. And yet, because I was "only" knocked out for less than 15 seconds, the official diagnosis was that I had a "mild" concussion. Yikes.

Takeaways about Concussions

There are so many concussion stories. Here are a few things I've learned about concussions:

- Accept every bit of medical help they will give you. Have them run every test to know what you're dealing with. See any specialist they recommend. And know you will likely reach your out-of-pocket maximum on your health insurance plan.
- The first hours and days are vital. Do everything your medical team tells you to do. Their instructions will likely include the following: do not look at your phone or computer, do not read, rest as much as possible, and always have someone with you, at least for the early days.
- Ask for help. If you are not used to asking for help, get over it. You will likely need help (my help included needing my face wiped as I vomited two days after the fall, having just arrived home from the hospital and wanting to go back because I was so miserable).
- Ask whoever is taking care of you to read up on anything else you can do (remember, you are not allowed to read). My life coach at the time recommended a book about concussions (see the Resources section starting on

page 260, and note, *Concussion Repair Manual*), which I had one friend order to send to another friend who had the time to (and did) read it end-to-end and then tell me the important bits.

- If you get periodic vertigo after a concussion, ask your neurosurgery team about Benign Positional Paroxysmal Vertigo (BPPV). I put this in here because it was months after my fall before I learned of it. Given the simple way BPPV can often be resolved, I wish I had known and had those months back.

- Get a dilated eye test after any hit to your head. I learned eight months after my fall, during a routine eye checkup, that I had a hole in one retina that may very well have come from the fall. My eye doctor said you should always get a dilated eye test after a fall to be safe.

Be Clear on Your Values, Boundaries, and Objectives

Taking the time upfront to work through your values and boundaries associated with horses is worth it. I define "values" as what is fundamentally important to you; that is, what makes your heart sing and feeds your soul. "Boundaries" are what you are willing and able to dedicate to this endeavor; this includes time, emotional energy, physical capacity, and money. "Objectives" describe where you think you are headed and will be constrained by your boundaries. You will revisit these things periodically, but reflecting on them early will keep you grounded.

The equestrian machine will encourage you to drift along the traditional path once you start. This generally includes starting with lessons to build a foundation, trying a bit of local showing, having your own horse in some way (whether a half-lease or purchase), and eventually spending all (and often more) of your liquid assets and disposable income on horses. And once you start, it is very easy to get caught up in it. That is not a bad thing *per se*, as long as you don't ignore your previously-defined boundaries when you make commitments. Here are some questions to ask yourself when pondering your values, boundaries, and objectives.

VALUES

What parts of horses or the horse world have captivated you? A few to contemplate:

- The absolute majesty of horses…their presence, physical awesomeness, and general nature of goodness.
- Your best friend is doing it and seems to have so much fun.
- The opportunity to learn…about horsemanship, riding, competing, and more.
- Wanting a new way to get physical exercise.
- The opportunity to compete.
- New social circles with amazing, grounded people.
- A place to bring my dog for outside time (warning on this one: many barns do not allow dogs off leash, if they are allowed at all).
- A mental break from daily life and responsibilities.
- The gear for you…regardless of your chosen discipline, the outfits are fabulous!

Which aspects are relatively more important to you?

- Being around horses, or riding horses?
- Learning to care for and groom horses, or riding horses tacked up for you?
- Riding, or also showing?
    - » One must ride, practice, and take many lessons before showing, but having a showing objective can focus the mind during all of your riding. Alternatively, you may not be interested in showing at all, which is also a lovely answer.
- Building a relationship with one horse, or engaging with different ones?
- Taking lessons in a group, or alone?
- Being at a highly social barn, or one that is less so?
- Being around mainly people your age, or open to a wide variety?
- Building new significant friendships, or finding fun barn acquaintances?

BOUNDARIES

Time:

- How much time can you dedicate per month, week, and day? (Remember, this must include travel time, working with your horse, riding your horse, and "barn time," the elusive suck of time where horse activities and chats about horses make hours disappear).

- Which days of the week and times of day work best? (For example, can you only ride after 6 p.m. on weekdays and weekends? Is Monday your most flexible day, only for you to learn that most barns in your area are closed that day?)

- Do you regularly travel such that you will be away for significant periods? How long are those periods generally (days or weeks)?

Emotional energy:

- How easily do you fall in love with animals? (This question matters because once you fall in love, you may ignore your original time and money boundaries).

- How much do you stress about animals in your world if they are in pain? (Is it all-consuming, or can you handle it without being distracted from all else?)

- How much do you stress about what other people think? (Will you burn emotional calories when the whole barn sees you have a terrible lesson, or watches you proudly walk into the ring only to be told you have your tack on wrong? Will you be bothered when you overhear petty barn members critiquing nearly everything about you and, even worse, your horse?)

- If tragedy strikes (for example, a horse you love must be retired early or—the ultimate tragedy—dies or needs to be put down), how much will that set you back, and can you handle that in your life right now?

Physical capacity:

- Can you physically handle the horse work and riding you would like? (Do you have limitations that are either normal to your body or due to other commitments that require physical exertion?)

- Are you able to ride regularly enough, or exercise to supplement, to improve your overall fitness? (Though not required, as stated previously on page 29, it will help you improve your riding.)

Money:

- How much of your income can you safely dedicate to horses? (See Chapter 3 starting on page 47 for how to estimate the various costs.)

- As you think about it today (before you fall in love with that perfect horse), how much of your savings are you willing to spend on your new horse habit?

- How many expensive surprises can you realistically pay for without dipping further into savings and risking other life plans?

OBJECTIVES

You can periodically fill out the following statements—and any additional ones you decide are important to you—to help you crystalize your objectives.

It is my objective to:

- Spend an average of _____ hours per week at the barn.
  - » Come to the barn an average of _____ times per week during the week, with my best days and time of day being _____.
  - » Come to the barn an average of _____ times per week on the weekend, with my best days and time of day being _____.

- Spend an amount of money that fits in my budget; this includes:
  - » Spend no more than _____ for up-front expenses (gear).
  - » Spend no more than _____ per year for additional purchases (gear).
  - » Spend no more than _____ per month for general expenses.
  - » Spend no more than _____ per year for showing.

- Achieve my broad vision for my riding:
  - » Describe your top values—for example, potentially, you want to enjoy time with horses and get comfortable with them over time, wherever that leads you; or you have a vision of showing in some manner.

- Progress my horsemanship and riding in the following way:
  - » Learn the first level of horsemanship in _____ months.
  - » Be comfortable at walk and trot in _____ months, and at canter in _____ months.

It is my objective to:

» Be able to ride on my own at the barn in _____ months.

» Be able to go on trail rides with others in _____ months.

» Go to my first show for the basics in _____ months.

» Reset my objectives in _____ months, then repeat the above exercise, going to intermediate levels and beyond, with more refinement around showing if that is one of my objectives.

Be Firm on Your Objectives, Yet Open to Feedback

Once you are clear on your values, boundaries, and objectives, you have something helpful to share with prospective trainers or your chosen trainer. You can take them through all your thinking or summarize your objectives. If you have had lots of conversations with horse people before this time (see the section on page 16) and received feedback on your thinking, you may have a reasonable set of objectives. If, however, you have done this exercise all on your own (not optimal, but fine!), then be prepared; the professionals may have to help you adjust your objectives to something more realistic. They should not tell you the only way to solve the problem is to spend more money, but they are well within their rights to say that given the time and money you can commit, your horsemanship and riding objectives are perhaps optimistic in the timeframe you specified.

Learning to be with horses, care for them, and ride them takes time. If you are a beginner and can take two group lessons a month, it will take you longer to develop than someone who can commit to one private and two group lessons per week. Both paths are beautiful and worth it; rely on your professional to help you refine your objectives to be achievable within your boundaries. If you stay firm on your boundaries and objectives, just be aware that the time it takes to reach your vision may be a bit longer than you hoped (elapsed time is often the variable that gets adjusted when setting expectations with a professional).

Consider the Time, Energy, and Financial Requirements

Chapter 3 starting on page 47 is dedicated to better understanding and preparing for the costs associated with your impending horse involvement. You will hear about the costs from almost anyone you talk with about horses. Unless you have grown up with and around horses, I promise you will be surprised at what some things cost.

You Will Spend More on Horseshoes than on Tires for Your Car

Recently, I was talking about how thoughtful I had been in getting good mileage out of the tires of my car, researching the best tires for the money, and subsequently spending about $1,200 for a complete set of tires to replace my existing ones, which had been showing their age at five years and 50,000 miles. It then struck me as ironic that I no longer think twice about paying $250–600 for a set of shoes for each of my horses every month (and the range in price can be more extensive depending on your geography and discipline). To summarize the paradox: an 8-year-old SUV costs ~$240/year for "shoes," while a horse can cost ~$2000–7000/year for their actual shoes.

I included this small horseshoe story for the shock factor, so that you will take Chapter 3 starting on page 47 seriously. Whether money is tight or flowing for you, you will benefit from gaining an understanding early. If money is tight, you will be in a better position to think deeply about how far you can go into the horse world (also see the section called "You Have Limited Money, and Want to Join the Horse World Economically," on page 253). If money is flowing, you will be able to prioritize how you spend and avoid overspending when it seems everyone's hand is out every step of the way (also see the section called "You Have Plenty of Money, and Do Not Want to Be Swindled," on page 254).

Find Your Power on This Journey

When you are new in the horse world, it can feel like everybody else knows more, and you must always defer to their recommendations. Indeed, some professionals prefer that you do as they say and don't bother them with your pesky newcomer questions. But you have both the agency and the obligation to take care of yourself and any horse you are responsible for. You do not need to be strident when you don't know much (asking questions with humility is always a good approach), but you have the right to make informed decisions for yourself and your horse.

Be Curious and Ask Questions to Build Your Expertise

At the beginning of your time with horses, you will likely follow the counsel of your professionals most of the time, if not all of the time. But before doing so, it is constructive to ask reasonable, probing questions to ensure you feel you are making an informed decision rather than simply deferring to whatever is recommended. This process is vital to building your knowledge and skills. When you do this for a while, your questions will become more nuanced, and you can start to add more value to the conversation.

As noted in the section starting on page 189, if you really do not have the time to do more than ask the basics, that is fine—if you are able to "trust yet verify" by using the Horse Care Plan starting on page 218 and keeping a watchful eye. You can monitor your horse when you are there, and perhaps ask barn friends to keep an eye on him as well. If you engage your friends to help, it is both polite and constructive to make it public knowledge that your friends are also checking on your horse.

Engaging with Professionals... Your Responsibilities and Rights

As you engage with your professionals, know that you have certain responsibilities to uphold and also certain rights you should feel comfortable asserting.

RESPONSIBILITIES

- Ask your questions thoughtfully and professionally. Even if something seems awry (and you believe someone at the barn messed up), starting with a "presumption of positive intent" will prevent an unnecessarily strained conversation.

- Work hard to remember the professionals' responses to your (prior many) questions and what they have told you (so they don't have to repeat themselves excessively).

- Uphold your commitments. That is, uphold your part in whatever is agreed as the plan.

RIGHTS

- Ask why things are done a certain way (for example, asking if anything seems odd to you related to how the barn is run, how you are treated, and how your horse is treated).

- Ask for an explanation of why something was done differently than discussed and agreed.

- Ask whether you are progressing in your horsemanship and riding as well as they might expect (and periodically ask for three things you are doing well and three things you could do better).

- Ask any question about your horse's care (for example, any element of the Horse Care Plan).

- Ask what else might be done to make your horse happier and healthier today and in the long term (general care, training, tack, feed, supplements, and so on).

At some point in your journey with horses, you will develop strong principles and opinions about nearly everything related to you and your horse. This can even apply to engaging with the top professionals with whom you interact. Finding your power starts with remembering these general rules of engagement:

- **Trainer**: You do not know how to ride or train as well as they do, but you know your body, how you (or your child) learn, and (eventually) your horse. You can ask why certain exercises are being used, what else you can do to improve your riding, why you are ineffective in certain exercises and effective in others, and so on.

- **Farrier**: You do not know anything about properly shoeing a horse, but you can ask things like: How are my horse's feet? What kind of shoes are you using and why? Does he need a hoof supplement? Why and which one? Do we have the right schedule for his shoeing? Would foot X-rays help you shoe him better?

- **Shipper**: This is one of my favorites. You do *not* have a right to heckle your shipper every hour of your horse's journey, nor to scream and yell if weather or traffic holds them up. But you should understand the journey plan and periodically check to see how it's going. When you are new to this, and sometimes forever, shippers prefer to engage with your trainer rather than you. See this as self-preservation on their part (considering the potential for hourly heckling from several owners), not as a reflection of how much they care about every horse on their truck (as repeated in many parts of this book about those working in the horse world, they love horses, too).

- **Vet**: More on this in the section starting on page 203, but know you have an absolute right to make the final decision before your horse is treated in any way. If you can't be there when the vet comes or are not reachable, give pre-approval for what you would be okay with, and other than that, treatment will have to wait (except for emergencies, and you should define and document, per page 105, who makes decisions for you in that case). As much or more than other professionals, vets frequently prefer to engage with the trainers and managers in your barn. This is mainly for the sake of efficiency, and sometimes they don't want to deal with too many more personalities. If you are okay with this approach, that is fine—but, again, know you have every right to talk with the vet directly. If you do so, you will get a lot more out of the conversation (and annoy the vet less) if you are prepared with questions, and you pay attention and take notes.

Finding your power in this new role as a horse person and horse parent requires curiosity, humility, strength, and gratitude. You are…

- Curious about everything and keen to learn each step of the way.
- Humble as a horse-loving neophyte.
- Strong in your commitment to do right by yourself, your child, and your horse, even if you offend or disgruntle humans in the process.
- Grateful to every person helping you in this new endeavor, and every horse you meet.

Be Gentle with Yourself on This Journey

Accept Responsibility for Your Role in This Journey

When you own your power, that includes accepting full responsibility for every decision you make, everything you do, and anything you do not do (inaction matters). And yet, you will make mistakes—and you must own those mistakes, whether you were acting on your own, based on an agreement with your trainer, or contrary to a professional's advice.

It can be gut-wrenching to digest that you made a mistake that was not good for—or even harmed—your horse in some way. You should review what happened and what you learned for the future. Sometimes, you might not change your overall approach, as nobody could have foreseen the situation. In other cases, you have new information to help you and everyone involved to do better by your horse next time.

Be Gentle with Yourself Along the Way To Give Yourself a Chance to Grow

With each mistake, you must work to be gentle with yourself. You and your horse care team (discussed in Chapter 6 starting on page 184) are trying your best and working with the resources available. Forgive yourself anything you believe you didn't get right, and vow to do better. But mostly, recognize that mistakes happen, and your main job is to get the vast majority of the big things right. Holding yourself to the standard of perfection is counter-productive and crazy-making.

- A few mental reminders on the subject of being good to yourself:
  - » You are here because you choose to be, and are grateful for every bit of it.
  - » You deserve to be here, and can do it on your own terms.
  - » Some days are harder than others, and this doesn't have to ruin your mood around or time with any horse with whom you come in contact.
  - » Your ride almost always feels worse than it looked (so use video).
- See the later section on the psychology of working with authority figures (for example, trainers) in the horse world (page 238).
- Be patient with your progress, especially if you are not riding regularly.
- You will progress, then plateau, then go backward, then progress twice as far…be intentional, pay attention, and be gentle with yourself on this glorious journey.
- If you have ridden before and are restarting after many years…
  - » Think of yourself as going back to ground zero. It will be slower to start over with all the foundational elements, but it will pay dividends later and allow you to accelerate faster.
  - » Remove any negative self-talk from prior years, take out any vocabulary about being "old" (even when you are in a lesson with a bunch of kids), and focus on the joy of this new path.

If you love horses, you belong here. You will find your way, own your power, and learn to be gentle with yourself. Good horse people will help you along the way. And the greatest listeners and counselors, horses, will be with you every step of the way. Perhaps even more than you know yourself, horses can feel your intention to do right by them. *They are rooting for you, and they are depending on you.*

Chapter Three

Understand the Financial Costs, Before You Ride Too Far

Who Would Have Budgeted for Two Saddles in One Year?

I stared at my beautiful saddle, the one I had bought new six months previously, bewildered about the news I had just received. Not only did I need to buy yet another saddle due to my horse's newly discovered back issues, but it would be a long shot to get even half of what I paid for the one in my possession.

I have had many financial shocks in my time with horses, the most predictable being medical treatments. This was a new one. I had spent thousands of dollars, was unlikely to recoup much of that, and had to spend another big chunk of money if I wanted my horse to have a chance at feeling good again in his body—not even a guarantee, but his best possible chance.

In this chapter, when I discuss adding contingencies to your financial plans, this story is part of the reason why. Though I eventually sold the first saddle for about 60 percent of what I had paid, it took years. In the meantime, my budget had gone out the window, and all I could do was suck up having to pay interest on the card used for the unplanned purchase (that or possibly risk contributing to having to retire the horse earlier than I had hoped).

Be Ready to Do Right by the Horses in Your Life

My objective is to help you start this journey with a full understanding of the potential time, energy, and financial costs associated with each step you take into the horse world. From volunteering (where the only cost, hopefully, is just the gas money to get you there) up to full ownership (where the numbers can be shocking), being prepared helps you manage your finances and fulfill your responsibilities when the unexpected happens. This chapter describes a view of the costs as of 2024. You can do the math yourself with the worksheets below or visit my website for a helpful calculator (www.andreasinner.com). I will update that online calculator periodically to reflect a more current view of the costs, and/or enhance it with a cost-of-living adjustment.

Whether you have modest funds available or a shedload, I do not know of any newcomer to the horse world who has not been periodically surprised and upset by large bills and unexpected costs. The only difference is that the person with more money can weather the shock without impacting their lifestyle, while the other may be presented with substantive life choices to make in order to do right by the horse. Sometimes, the surprises result from a barn not being sufficiently transparent about things. Other times, your horse suddenly needs a special anything (gear, treatment, and so on) that you've never heard of before. And, most unfortunately, there are also times when it is a medical issue that sends your finances into turmoil (see the section starting on page 106 for more on the topic of insurance for the big-ticket items).

Over the years, I have often been extended beyond my original "plan." I hope this information helps you be less surprised than I was along the way.

The Cost of Beginning to Be Around Horses

Early Costs and Sourcing Options

The table below provides an inventory of required items and suggestions for when to borrow them from your barn or buy them yourself. These designations are illustrative, given every barn is different; ask the question and know that almost every barn structure (though not necessarily pricing) is reasonable. If it's a barn that caters to newcomers, they will tend to offer more of these items; if it's a barn that only has horses owned by individuals (no lesson horses), they will tend to expect you to bring everything you need (and given that includes bringing a horse, this is not a candidate for your first barn).

Whenever possible, try to borrow—or even better, have gifted to you—any of the items. Hand-me-downs are wonderful because they not only save you money, but also make someone else feel good about giving their unused items a second life. Also note that anywhere that specifies "buy" does not mean "buy new" (other than safety equipment like helmets and vests). There are amazing consignment stores and online marketplaces where you can find what you need without paying list prices for new items. As with any new hobby, keep your initial costs to a minimum until you are sure you are enthralled and want to keep going; otherwise, you will be the one trying to sell your essentially brand-new items on the marketplace as you go off to find another hobby.

Cost Description	You Are Lessoning	You Lease/Own
Gear for you		
• Breeches (or leggings, or jeans)	• Gift/Buy	• Gift/Buy
• Boots (paddock or riding)	• Borrow/Buy	• Gift/Buy
• Chaps (half or full, depends on discipline)	• Optional	• Optional
• Helmet (careful with hand-me-downs)	• Borrow/Buy	• Buy
• Safety vest (careful with hand-me-downs)	• Borrow/Buy	• Buy
• Special shirts (sun protection is vital)	• Not needed	• Gift/Buy
• Special underwear, socks, and belts	• Not needed	• Optional
• Tack trunk*	• Not needed	• Optional
Lessons/training		
• Lessons	Pick your model from the available options.	Pick your model from the available options.
• Lesson packages		
• Full training		
Board		
• Dry stall	n/a	Pick from these three model options (and potentially variations).
• Regular board	n/a	
• Full care	n/a	
Gear for your horse		
• Halters and leads	Barn should have everything in this category for you.	Typically buy, but find ways to borrow or have gifted as much as possible along the way. A leased horse should come with some of his gear.
• Blankets, sheets, fly sheets, and fly masks		
• Boots and wraps		
• Bridles and headstalls		
• Reins and bits		
• Saddles		
• Saddle pads and half pads		
• Stirrups and stirrup leathers		
• Girths and girth covers		
• Training gear (lunge line, etc.)		

Cost Description	You Are Lessoning	You Lease/Own
Grooming gear for your horse • Hoof pick • Curry combs and grooming mitts • Brushes (endless!) • Mane and tail brushes • Cleaning and grooming products (endless!)	Barn should have everything in this category for you.	The barn may have them available, but buying your own keeps it hygienic, and you will have favorites.
Medical supplies for your horse • Bandages, vet wrap, and so on (wound care and protection) • OTC infection treatments • Anti-inflammatories (including for colic) • Pain relievers • Thrush treatment • …endless list, but ask what you should get yourself	Barn should have everything in this category for you.	Periodic use is typically covered in board, but do ask. If you will be using something every day, you should get your own supply.
Feed and supplements • Hay • Feed • Supplements	All covered by the barn.	Typically covered in board, except for supplements and any specialty feed for just your horse.

---

*   I do not recommend brands in this book. But I do recommend that you use your favorite search engine to find black plastic 50-gallon or 63-gallon rolling trunks at ~$100. I have spent too much money over the years on fancy wood tack trunks (including with special colors at each new barn) when these plastic rolling ones are functional, durable, and far easier to transport.

Gear for You

If you are just at the stage of considering taking lessons, be careful how much you spend on gear and yet also enjoy every moment of shopping for it. As noted above, spend as little as you can until you know this is the sport for you (use consignment shops, online marketplaces, and so on). Indeed, if you've found the right horsey people, you can probably borrow just about everything to start (if not from your barn, then from a friend or friend-of-a-friend).

And yet, for the things you need and can't find a way to borrow, spend as much time as you like asking for advice, shopping, trying on, and eventually purchasing. All the time you spend discussing and surfing educates you. It teaches you what you find appealing and, of course, what the sport generally views as currently "normal" or "in fashion." Go online and also arrange to have physical catalogs delivered. Being with horses is your destination, but every preparatory step is good fun. Let the horse world amaze and wash over you. In my early days, I had a stack of horse catalogs on my bedside and coffee tables—and still today, I find the variety of items simply amazing.

A special note here about helmets and safety vests: This is one area where you should not scrimp. Ever. You may ride in a discipline where neither are used, but I'm not budging from my recommendation. You can ignore me if you are comfortable taking the risk.

In the section starting on page 30, I talk about safety generally and my personal experience with concussions. There are too many stories of experienced riders having accidents while walking or even while getting on their horse. The technology of safety items is getting better and better, so take advantage. And whether anyone in your barn thinks it's "cool" or not, buy and use a safety vest. The top riders in certain disciplines are wearing vests more and more. Be cool like them!

It may surprise you, but you can always spend more than even the "High" of the range in the tables below, and thus the "(+ on up)" in the title. Sometimes that intergalactic pricing is due to customization (for example, custom boots are helpful for certain body types), and sometimes it is just fancy.

Cost Description	Low	High (+ on up)
Gear for you		
• Breeches	• $40	• $600
• Boots	• $50	• $1000
• Chaps	• $50	• $500
• Helmet	• $50	• $900
• Safety vest	• $100	• $900
• Special shirts	• $25 each	• $300 each
• Special underwear, socks, belts	• $10 each	• $200 each
• Tack trunk	• $100	• $1000

Lessons

If you are a newcomer, you will start with lessons. Perhaps you've been on some vacation trail rides, but lessons are always the first step—walk away if someplace offers to put you on a horse without supervision. Depending on what your barn offers, I suggest several one-on-one lessons ("private") at the start. If you can't afford that, just ensure your group lessons have people close to your newbie level.

I also suggest you take lots of lessons before you ride alone. Your barn will likely enforce this suggestion (which is to say they won't let you ride alone on a lesson horse until they are comfortable with your abilities), so know this is normal. This approach is productive for your riding and essential for your safety—that is, it is not just because they want lots of lesson dollars from you.

Start with whatever frequency fits your schedule and budget (for example, once a week or twice a month) and then slowly find your way. Starting on page 242, I talk about how to get the most out of your lessons.

Lesson Category	Potential Cost
Private lesson	$50–200/hour
Group lesson	$40–100/hour
Lesson package (discount for multiple purchased at once)	(some barns offer this)
Clinics (outside trainers)	$100–1000/day
Specialized coaching (outside trainers)	$75–500/hour

Early Shows and Competitions

In the early stages of your riding, you may be offered the chance to participate in a show at your barn or close by. There are classes for all levels at these wonderful typically un-rated shows, and you should take advantage of them if the idea appeals to you. As a newcomer, these early shows are less about competition and more about meeting other horse people and having a new type of experience with your horse (whether it be a lesson horse or your horse).

Cost Description	Potential Cost
Use of lesson horse per class (or per day)	$25–75/class ($50–300/day)
Entry fee per class	$25–100/class
Coaching fee per class	$25–100/class
Grooming (if this applies)	$30–100/day
Braiding (if this applies)	$25–100 (mane and tail)
Shipping (if not at your home barn)	$1–3/mile (or there may be a flat fee, unrelated to miles, for a short trip)
Splits (any costs spread out among those participating)	Ask your barn
Ask if there are any other fees before you sign up	Ask your barn

The Massive Shift When You Lease or Buy a Horse

In my corporate career, I had many colleagues with children who wanted to ride or had started to ride. Since I became involved with horses, I have made a great many friends with the parents of juniors with whom I was riding or taking lessons. And, of course, I have known many people who were starting to ride themselves.

I repeat here what I have said to every one of them, whether they asked or not, about whether horses are a good idea:

- **Go for it!** When horses speak to you, there is no better source of fulfillment, growth, and exercise than building a life with them. For young people especially, they will learn about responsibility, discipline, community, and love in a gorgeous way (though note the cautions I share in the sections starting on page 25 and page 232 about potential peer pressure and the risks of abuse respectively). … AND …
- **Hold off on leasing or buying.** Stay with lesson horses as long as you can stand it, until you know you have fallen in love with horses and your chosen discipline. Once you lease or buy a horse, the floodgates will open in terms of your time, energy, and financial commitments. Whenever possible, start with leasing before buying.

Deciding to lease or buy a horse is a life-changing event. The process of finding a horse can be educational and fun, yet it also frequently comes with periodic heartbreaks (for example, that mare you adore who is, amazingly, in your price range, has enough red flags from the pre-purchase exam that you need to walk away). If, after working through this chapter, you know you can afford it, congratulations! Starting in Chapter 4 on page 112, I describe how to find a barn and a team; that, of course, should be done before you consider buying a horse. Starting on page 158, I describe the horse shopping process.

In this chapter, my entire objective is to give you a sense of all the costs so you can decide whether you want to go down this road. If you start shopping before you know for sure you can afford it, you may fall in love with a horse and convince yourself you can make it work. This is a dangerous approach, so please work through the content below before you go too far and end up over-extended (albeit with heart-felt positive intentions).

Something to Know: You Will Spend Huge $, but (Almost) Nobody Is Getting Rich

This financial reality of the horse world has been difficult for me to comprehend over the years. I have many friends who are barn owners, show owners, trainers, vets, chiropractors, acupuncturists, farriers, grooms, owners, and riders, and they have all educated me in one way or another. I have learned that even though it can feel like everyone has their hand out and you're spending more in a week or month than you ever dreamed (and that may actually be true), almost nobody is getting rich off you. Except in some situations—which include but are not limited to professionals helping to buy and sell very expensive horses (and thus earning large commissions), elite medical professionals, and the small few who work hard to rip you off—everyone else is barely making ends meet.

Barns Are Complicated and Expensive to Run

Barns are astonishingly expensive to run. Hiring and keeping quality barn staff is difficult and costly, especially in recent years. The mobile nature of the show world, when that applies to you, has inherent, substantive costs (travel, housing, meals without a kitchen, and so on). There are providers for every element of the horse world (braiders, shippers, medical, shows, and more), and they all work to stay busy to pay next month's rent or mortgage. The ones who run their own business must manage their staff (facilities, payroll, insurance, overheads) and provision for the ups and downs of the business. The years of the pandemic had disastrous effects on many of these businesses, and some are still recovering.

I will never defend bad actors in the horse world; they do exist, and I will discuss them in the next section and a bit more starting on page 167. But when you start this journey, do so with the presumption of positive intent. Most everyone working in the horse industry is passionate about horses and is simply trying to earn a decent living that allows them to be close to the animals they love.

Have Some Grace When You Ask about Prices and Bills

You should not overpay or double-pay (as is sometimes the case with hidden commissions) and should check everything. But when the bills are beyond your expectations, check your assumptions and your math before you presume someone is trying to rip you off. And then ask your questions based on the facts rather than based on a story you have spun up about your trainer/vet/farrier suddenly being evil (or the amplified story when you decide they've been evil all along and you've been a sucker). If anyone did something wrong, most of the time, their worst sin is being a poor communicator—there is a lot of that in the horse world. Poor communication is not acceptable, but unless it is intentional, it isn't nefarious. In scenarios where you have a legitimate basis to guess at bad intent, I discuss that in the sections below.

Something Else to Know: Some People May Waste or Take More of Your Money Than They Deserve

My message in the prior section is that most people running a business in the horse world are barely squeaking by, but this section discusses the darker side. Before I start with a parade of horribles: if you receive a large bill from any professional that includes services and products you and your horse indeed received and were charged for aligned with the price sheet you were provided (or aligned with normal pricing in your area), that does not qualify as someone doing a bad thing. That goes in the category of this endeavor sometimes being an expensive one. Some months can be surprising.

Also consider that barns are fairly public places with many clients with varying degrees of experience and sophistication. It is very rare for systemic fraud or malfeasance to be operating in any kind of horse service business you will encounter in your early days without someone before you sniffing it out. You should receive the same price sheet that everyone else has, read your bills every month, and promptly and politely ask whoever sends you the bills any questions. Your being disciplined and attentive—including paying said bills on time—will help you in the long run.

The bigger financial danger comes into play when you start leasing or buying horses. This is due to the scale of money, small number of people involved, and one-off nature of the transactions—it is easier to hide a single private lie than a repetitive public one. Accordingly, in addition to some of the items included in this section below, there are further recommendations for how to protect yourself in the acquisition process on pages 167-75.

Management Practices May Lead to More Costs for You

Most professionals are disciplined in how they run their businesses; they are excellent with published price sheets, rigorous accounting, and timely billing. But those who are less so can end up costing themselves, their business, and their clients more money. This can be annoying, and you have a right to ask them to be more disciplined, but it doesn't mean there is anything nefarious. And yet it can still impact your cash flow, and so a few things to watch out for are below.

- **Billing several months of an item in one bill.** If any service provider forgets to add an item for several months and then "catches up" all at once, it is a hit to your assumed costs generally and your cash flow that month.
  - » If the item is legitimate, discuss a payment plan—their poor administrative skills should not create an emergency on your part. If it is a complete surprise to you generally, that is when it is time to sit down to review the price sheet with whoever is in charge of such things.

- **Adding hidden fees for the care of your horse.** I had one barn surreptitiously markup all the vet charges, which they insisted be billed through them; the concept itself isn't necessarily bad (and thus why I have this in the bad management bucket rather than further down), but the attempt to keep it hidden always is.
  - » Especially for a large barn, it is quite helpful to service providers such as farriers and shippers to not have to chase all the clients separately. Your barn is providing a valuable service to them when they consolidate the bills, so do not presume "pass-through" is equal to nefarious. Simply make sure you understand the math.
- **Requiring the use of certain providers in return for (sometimes) undisclosed kickbacks.** There has always been, and will always be, small businesses helping each other; those types of synergies and arrangements are not my concern. Where the line can be crossed is a barn insisting on something that may not even be needed just to keep the deal going.
  - » If you wonder if your horse really needs something or whether it is being offered at a reasonable market rate, talk with your trainer and do some research.
- **Making clients who do show cover the costs of clients who cancel at the last minute.** This is not a barn or trainer trying to make more; it is typically a failure to enforce reasonable cancellation policies, such that the good egg clients end up paying more because of the bad eggs.
  - » Ask about the policies for canceling your participation in any event or show. That is, the last day you can let your barn know that you're not going without having to incur cancellation fees or even paying for everything, including your reserved stalls, your portion of shared stalls, your portion of the groom charges, and so on.
- **Adding more to the "splits" (costs shared across clients showing) than expected.** When you see a show bill, it will have a portion of costs

split across everyone from your barn and may include grooming stalls, shavings, and so on; if it includes a lot more, such as the stalls for all the professionals' horses, you have a right to inquire in a polite way without getting your head bitten off.

> » Ask in advance what you can expect to see on this part of the bill and ensure that you are okay with it (both in principle and financially) before you go to the show.

Poor Horse Matching Can Be Very Costly…Yet It Is Art and Science

The section on the topic of horse shopping, starting on page 158, is long because finding the right horse at the right time is challenging. Your trainer is incented to find you a good horse, one that will make you happy and keep you growing in your equestrian addiction/passion. They will tap into all their resources to get this done. And yet sometimes, the outcome isn't the nirvana you imagined.

- **Finding you a horse for too much money.** The pricing of horses is complicated, as often the value is in the eye of the beholder…and it is easy to convince people to spend more after they have fallen in love with a horse.
  - » Have the nerve to walk away if you think the horse is priced too high, even after negotiation, and definitely walk away if you can't afford it.
  - » If you suspect the price is inflated, verify that other buyers are being quoted the same price. Yes, different buyers, with varying levels of wealth, will be quoted different prices…just like the same model of pool heater mysteriously costs more in some neighborhoods.
- **Finding you a horse for too little money.** The point here is that a horse might not be a great match for very long; if you spend a bit more, you could save money in the long run by buying the right horse the first time rather than having to buy and sell multiple times…and paying the commissions each time.

- **Finding you a horse that ends up being a poor match or not fit for his intended job.** Everyone involved can have the best intentions and do all the right things, and still things do not turn out well. Any time the outcome isn't optimal, you should sit down with your professional to discuss whether there was anything anyone would do differently next time. You might learn something in this process. Or you might be stuck with reflections like "maybe this horse doesn't love this new job I gave him," "maybe his many competitive years before I bought him are finally catching up with him and he just can't hold up to the job at his age," or "maybe he's still a fantastic horse but he and I simply aren't a great match."

Poor Horse Care Practices Can Impact Your Horse's Health, and Your Financials

Every service provider in your horse care team, especially your barn, plays a role in keeping your horse happy, healthy, and sound. If anyone involved—no matter how senior or junior—does not do their job well, bad things can happen. There are a thousand and one things that can happen to these beautiful creatures—let alone all the things they can do to themselves. This entire book is designed to help you do right by them. That objective is not only important for the sake of your horse; running a tight ship will also save you money in the long run. As the saying goes in the process consulting world (leveraged from Joseph Malin's 1895 poem), "Better [to] put a strong fence 'round the top of the cliff / Than an ambulance down in the valley." That is, disciplined prevention is less painful and costly than fixing avoidable problems later (and leaves you with cash to spare for whatever shows up that is unavoidable).

And Sometimes, There Is Downright Fraud Afoot

Sometimes people feel they deserve more of your money, for whatever reason, and they concoct ways to get it. The vast majority of people—honest and hardworking—are rightly and deeply frustrated by those who seem committed to giving the horse industry a bad name. But it is not going to disappear tomorrow, so you might as well have a hint on where to be wary.

- **Adding made-up fees and charges.** I love technology for many things, and that includes the ability to make beautiful documents. But creating a sexy looking PDF with whatever you want on it is quite simple these days. It is a bold person who will try to pass off such a thing, but it does happen.
  - » Check your bills. Ask for invoices for anything passed through to you. Check those as well.
- **Adding extra—and hidden—commissions.** Sometimes there are multiple professionals, trainers, and agents involved in the buying and selling of a horse, and it seems everyone has their hand out. Additional commissions can be fully legitimate, but nothing should be a surprise (not approved by you in advance) or hidden (fraud). A fraudulent element could also be in the form of a "kick-back," where your professional arranges for you to buy a horse from someone they know, who adds extra $$$ to the price they quote you, and they share the spoils, which is in addition to any agreed commission percentage you are already paying your professional directly.
  - » Whenever possible, email all parties with any relevant documentation such as horse passport, breeding, purchase and sale agreement, and bill of sale (to ensure everyone is seeing the same details along the way, and the same deal terms).
  - » Make sure the purchase and sale agreement indicates the buyer and seller are responsible for paying their respective commissions separately from the sales transaction (what the other party pays for commissions is none of your business).
  - » Such shenanigans can also occur in a lease situation. Keep a watchful eye.

- **Finding a horse for you they know you can't ride (it is really meant for them).** This will result in either a) you not having fun or being in danger, having to sell the horse, and then buying another and paying commissions for each transaction, and/or b) you having to pay your trainer to ride the horse all of the time rather than a reasonable once per week to keep the horse in good form.
  - » Talk with your trainer about why they think the horse is a good match.
  - » Do everything during your trial on the horse that you want to do; if you're not jumping yet and want a horse that can jump, ask that another amateur jump him rather than just your trainer (who can hopefully make any horse look good).
- **Finding a horse for you that isn't the horse on the paperwork.** This is outright fraud and is very rare given the help of breed registries, micro-chipping, show records, and social media.
  - » Work with your trainer to ensure the source is trusted and the paperwork matches.
  - » Do your own research on the horse via social media, USEF/equivalent, online videos, and so on; you don't have to be an expert to notice that a horse missed a year of showing in an otherwise regular showing schedule, and it's valid to ask about that and see if things generally line up. If anyone involved tells you to not bother with such research, do it anyway.

I must finish this longer-than-desired section with a reminder that not everybody is out to get you. In fact, very few people are. Most everybody in this industry loves horses, loves it when newcomers also find joy in being with horses, and runs a heartfelt honest business in service of all of that. Treat them well in return and you will have a wonderful time.

Cost Categories

The categories below are detailed in subsequent sections. There is also a worksheet available on my website (andreasinner.com).

- **Rehabilitation and Early Retirement** (this is listed first for a reason… humor me and read it, beginning on page 65)
- **Upfront Costs** (page 67)
  - » **Lease Price** (varied models—page 67)
  - » **Purchase Price** (page 68)
  - » **Pre-Purchase Exams** (applies to leases as well—page 69)
  - » **Commissions** (page 69)
  - » **Insurance** (mortality and theft, loss of use, major medical and surgical, private horse owner liability, air transit—page 69)
- **Ongoing Costs** (page 73)
  - » **Outfit Yourself and Your Horse** (this is both an upfront and an ongoing cost—page 73)
  - » **Develop Your Horse and Your Riding** (page 82)
    - **Training and Exercise** (for your horse when you're not the one exercising him—page 84)
    - **Gear for Training and Exercise** (whatever you can't borrow—page 85)
    - **Lessons** (for the days you want to take one—page 85)
  - » **Cover Regular and Exceptional Horse Care** (page 86)
    - **Board** (stall, turnout, hay, feed, potentially full care—page 86)
    - **Farrier** (keep in mind this is generally monthly—page 88)
    - **Veterinarians** (general, soundness, specialist, surgeon—page 89)
    - **Other Medical Care** (dentist, chiropractor, acupuncturist, masseuse—page 89)
    - **Special Feed and Supplements** (typically not covered in board—page 90)

» **Show and Compete** (page 91)
- **Show Fees and "Splits"** (page 92)
- **Shipping, Training, and Grooming** (page 94)
- **Tips and Gifts** (page 95)
- **Personal Travel** (page 96)

Rehabilitation and Early Retirement (This Is Listed First for a Reason)

You have found the horse of your dreams for you or your child. The trials (yes, plural) were amazing. You rode better than you ever have and felt a connection with the horse. Your trainer thinks he's perfect for you, and the vet found nothing unusual in the pre-purchase exam, let alone scary. The price is right, and you're satisfied with the commission structure, so…you have bought yourself a horse. Congratulations!

Note: If these terms are confusing, know there are more details about horse shopping starting on page 158, along with deep dives on "trials" (trying a horse) starting on page 165 and pre-purchase exams on page 166.

Sometimes, Bad Things Happen to Good Horses

You have no doubt guessed this story takes a turn. At some point early in your ownership, the horse gets hurt, gets sick, or goes off (is no longer sound and can't do his expected job) for any number of reasons. Regular care will sometimes get you back on track with your horse. In other scenarios, the horse needs extensive special medical treatment and then requires a) lengthy rehabilitation or b) retirement from his job of being your horse to ride or perhaps anybody's horse to ride.

I share this sad hypothetical because once you purchase a horse, all the possible paths forward from that point are your responsibility. Whether your horse becomes a lawn ornament for the rest of his natural life or needs time to get back to doing his job, it sits with you. Accordingly, when you decide to buy a horse, you should do so understanding that a dire situation like this is possible—far from likely, but possible.

You will recall my view of our responsibilities as humans and the rights of the horses in our lives in the section starting on page 19. Taking care of them in a situation like this is your responsibility. Presenting a cost illustration of rehabilitation and retirement is challenging as there can be many expenses. But consider the costs below, and then consider a horse could live until 30 or longer…that is your potential exposure.

Cost Description	Potential Cost (excluding vet and farrier costs)
General rehabilitation	$400–1000+/month
Specialty rehabilitation (confined turnout, regular special treatments, and so on)	$1000–2000+/month
General retirement	$250–600+/month
High-touch retirement	$500–1500+/month

You now understand why this section is very early in this chapter. If the numbers above have left your head spinning, then follow my earlier advice to take lessons or lease rather than buy.

Nobody But You Will Make Sure the Rest of This Horse's Life Is Good

If you own a horse and he needs to be suddenly retired—I repeat it here because it bears repeating—it is your job to take care of him. If, instead, you decide to abdicate your responsibility for this creature and off-load him somewhere, you have to recognize that his future may not be pretty. Once a horse no longer fits the human definition of "useful," it is quite likely terrible things will happen to him. Handing off the horse you bought and accepted responsibility for to a non-profit (or some other type of organization) to care for him at this juncture without conducting proper due diligence on that organization often leads to neglect, abuse, and (I am not being dramatic here) even slaughter.

There are some high-quality options for donating a horse who can only do less work than you had planned. For example, if your horse's jumping days are over and you really want to jump, there are amazing therapeutic riding programs where that horse could have a good life and do a job that is suited to him. However, it remains your responsibility to ensure his new life is a good one. You must verify that the adopting organization has a track record for fulfilling their (transferred from you) responsibilities and respecting the rights of the horse. And you should discuss with them how you can stay updated on his health and welfare over time.

Fancy horses who had incredible careers have ended up in kill pens. That is in addition to all the horses who might not be described as "fancy," but are still beautiful and yet tragically fill the neglect/abuse/slaughter pipeline every day.

In short, do not think it can't happen to your horse after you discard him.

Upfront Costs

The first theme of this section is to make it clear that though everyone must decide their budget, it is worth remembering that your monthly spending for board and training can quickly add up to and surpass your purchase price. So, though the initial financial hit is clearly hard to take, be careful you don't underbuy, as you will be paying just about the same for upkeep regardless of the purchase price. And yet, see the prior section for discussion of the fact that all horses are a risk (and herein lies one of the many sets of conflicting messages you need to digest in this wonderful world).

Half-Lease: One option that is a great next step beyond lessons on a school horse is a half-lease. They are not always available, but when they are, it is worth exploring. You will likely have to pay a fee of some sort and definitely a portion of expenses, and you typically have three days per week to be able to ride or take lessons on the horse. The other three days may be allocated to the lessor (the owner), or perhaps to another lessee. This model's brilliance is that it saves money and sometimes matches the time you can allocate to riding at this stage. The challenge of this model is working out who is allowed to do what with the horse (to ensure he is not overworked and yet still stays in shape) and how to allocate and adjust the days each rider has. When I talk with the parents of a horse-mad child who wants their own horse, I suggest doing everything you can to start with this model. Each ownership model beyond this one becomes exponentially more expensive.

Full Lease: The annual lease fee can run up to one-third or even one-half of the sale price (in addition to taking over expenses). That top end might sound crazy (why would I spend half of the sale price on a lease when I could own outright him in 2 years?!?), but sometimes you need a horse for a specific purpose and not beyond that—typically for kids in the juniors' path rather than adults. And remember, a lease means you are not responsible for him for the rest of his life.

Free Lease: In this model, though you do not have to pay a lease "fee," you still take on the responsibility for most or all expenses (or a portion of expenses if it is a "free half-lease"). There are fine horses who might be available through this model, so keep an eye and ear out for possibilities. I have used this model once when I was out of the country for an extended period. My horse stayed in my barn with my trainer, and a trusted capable friend took on some of the expenses in return for being able to ride him.

Purchase: The purchase price for a horse can also range from $0 (someone wants the horse off their payroll) up to millions. That is a very unhelpful range. But as prices depend on your geography, the discipline of riding you want to pursue, the kind of horse best suited to that discipline, and your aspirations in general, there is no way to give you a tighter range. I can't imagine a first purchase being a massive number, but it's not out of the question for someone who has leased for many years and wants to be a top competitor in certain disciplines.

Pre-Purchase Exam: When you intend to buy a horse, or even lease, get a qualified and objective vet (one who works for you and doesn't know the current owner) to complete a pre-purchase exam. This should include full X-rays, a soundness exam, a blood test, and a drug test. The drug test is to make sure your potential horse didn't have anything in his system on the day of the pre-purchase exam that might have made him appear sounder and saner. You can also ask the seller for vet records; they may or may not provide them, but either response tells you something. There is more on the topic of pre-purchase exams starting on page 166.

Commissions: This should be a simple topic. Unfortunately, this is an unregulated industry when it comes to commissions (there is nothing akin to the system governing commissions in the real estate world). When you buy or sell a horse, you should expect to pay your trainer, and possibly a broker or other involved professional, a commission. Can you buy a horse completely on your own? Possibly. But, especially in the early days, I would not recommend it. How much is the commission? I've seen everything from 0 percent (sometimes a trainer will "give away" their right to a commission just to get a particular deal done) on up to 10, 15, or even 20 percent. So, consider a simple transaction where you buy a $30,000 horse. You could end up paying the current owner $30,000, your trainer $4,500, and remember that you already paid the vet for the pre-purchase exam—and perhaps a couple preceding pre-purchase exams when you decided not to buy the horse in question, before you found this horse. For an illustration of this math, see the section starting on page 153.

Insurance: The section starting on page 106 includes ideas on the types of insurance you should consider. Talk with your current insurance agent and ask if any of your new horse-related activities and risks are covered or—quite important to know—excluded. Find an equine insurance agent and ask them about options that may go beyond what a traditional insurance provider can offer. Talk with your horsey friends about what insurance they have or don't have, and why. Making assumptions about insurance rarely works in your favor. Even if you decide against buying any insurance, you will at least know where you are exposed.

Decide on a Budget

Consider the Purchase Price a Sunk Cost If at All Possible

Though you might be able to later sell the horse and recoup some (hopefully, all, or, aspirationally, more) of your money, it is best to think of the purchase price as a completely sunk cost. Accordingly, your budget for purchase should be a cash outlay that you can live without. Forever. When I'm wrong about this, you will be pleasantly surprised. When I'm right, you will not be caught unawares.

Deciding on a budget is a bit of an iterative process. You should have a basic idea of how much money you can spend. You then talk with your trainer about a range of potential prices to make sure you're not kidding yourself. And then, the hard work on your side is to decide on what is a realistic, and hopefully conservative, amount of money you can budget for buying a horse.

Horse Shopping, Commissions, and Ongoing Care Are All Added on Top

The section starting on page 153 discusses scenarios involving the costs related to buying a horse, including expenses beyond the purchase price. The short answer is that if, for example, you're considering $20k the approximate "price" of the horse, you will likely spend closer to $28k to get the deal done (when you include vetting, commissions, shipping, insurance, new gear, and so on). So your budget should be at least $30k you are willing to remove from your liquid assets and put into an amazing, living, breathing, eating, pooping, and loving equine asset. And remember, that is just on day one. You then have the ongoing upkeep discussed in the sections starting on page 73.

Horse Pricing Is Goofy: A Couple Things to Know

The market dynamics in the horse world for buying and selling are mostly logical but also a little bit whacky. I consider a proper market one where the seller's price reflects the inherent value of the item, but with horses the value is in the eyes of the buying community. Where the horse world goes off the rails—and operates a bit like the market for fine art—is two main things: A) sellers commonly consider how much they have spent on the horse, believe they should be able to get that back, and price accordingly, and B) the seller or the middlemen (brokers, trainers, and so on) often adjust the price they quote to match how much money they believe the potential buyer has.

For scenario A, if the horse is worth what they are asking, that's fine. If the seller is trying to make up for their own buying mistake or inability to increase the horse's value commensurate with their ongoing investment, I believe that is their problem, not yours. Stay strong in your view of what a horse is worth to you and only you. Your trainer will likely need to explain what you can get within your budget (to help manage your expectations). But there is no need to overpay when the price is not justified to you. You may lose horses because of this approach, but you have a lower probability of overpaying, and, as with everything in this book, it is your choice whether to pay attention to this advice.

For scenario B, bluntly, there can be inflation on a price if someone in the mix thinks they can get away with it. For example, if some person in the middle knows of a $50k horse that will meet the buyer's needs and the buyer has said they can spend up to $100k, they may quote the price at $80k and pocket the difference. Sometimes they'll even let other professionals in on it, so everyone gets a piece of the action. The section starting on page 167 discusses how to avoid such scenarios by, for example, talking directly to the other party (where possible), putting everything in writing, and sharing the details with all parties involved.

Budget More than You Originally Imagined, But Don't Risk Your Lifestyle

But back to expectations. Whatever the price of the horse you end up buying, it will feel like a lot of money. And yet, most of the time, you will have bought the quality of horse that aligns with that dollar amount. If you want a fancy hunter that will win at top-rated shows, add a zero or two to whatever dollar amount you were thinking. Unicorns are very, very expensive. In every discipline.

Deciding on a budget range is like threading the tiniest of needles. You want to spend enough to get a horse you can learn from and one with whom you can grow together (see the section starting on page 153, which makes the point that it is an ongoing cost that is often what hurts the most, so don't scrimp on the purchase price). Yet you also don't want to overspend on a horse where it will take you years to grow into his capabilities. Only you can determine the budget where you are confident, comfortable, and generally relaxed about the whole thing. Armed with that number, your trainer can hunt for your match.

You Are Not Buying a Car…You Are Acquiring a
Living Creature to Be Your Partner

It is difficult to spend a shocking amount of money and then, a few weeks or months later, be surprised that the horse is not quite the creature you imagined he would be. If you bought a fancy car with certain specs and this happened, you would bring it back to the dealer and say, "It only does 0–60 in 5.7 seconds…I spent all that extra money for the model that would do 3.7 seconds!" (#FirstWorldProblems).

Unless you're dealing with an unusual situation and have a legitimate case for doing so, there are many reasons why you will not go back to the seller or broker:

- Your purchase and sale agreement and your bill of sale likely made it clear that you had a chance to vet and try the horse, and the seller did not guarantee anything about the horse's suitability for or future performance in his job.

- You have likely changed a lot in terms of how the horse is cared for, where he is living, how he is ridden, the energy of the barn, how much he is turned out, what he's eating, and so on…any of those things can impact performance.
- You may not be as good a rider or even simply as good a match for the horse as the prior rider. Sometimes you're a better match and can take the horse to bigger and better places, but you have to recognize there is a chance that if the horse is not performing as well as he was when you tried him…it is because of you.

Now that I've told you you're stuck, here is one helpful thing to know:

- It is *very* common to go backward for a little bit with a horse you just bought before you find your groove together. It is annoying, after amazing trial rides and spending all that money, but just know it happens, it can take 6 to 12 months to develop a true partnership, and stay positive.

Ongoing Costs

Outfit Yourself and Your Horse

This section describes much of the "gear" needed for this sport. You do not need to buy it all at once. However, it is good to know the full gamut of potential expenses, in part so you don't spend big early and run out of funds for important items. It is also good to understand the complete shopping list before you meander bright-eyed into your nearby tack shop (or worse, online, where literally everything is available); it is easy, and quite fun, to wander about (physically or virtually) and simply buy things that look cool and probably useful. The experience is akin to walking into Target for a "quick look" and spending far more than you planned on things you may never use. Starting on page 64, I share a summary of upfront and ongoing costs.

Acquire What You Know to Be Useful or Believe to Be Beautiful (Hopefully Both)

To begin, I share a quote that I believe applies to life generally and to everything in your acquisition choices (hand-me-downs, borrowed items, and purchases alike) in the horse world.

> *"Have nothing in your houses that you do not know to be useful or believe to be beautiful."*
>
> William Morris, 1834-1896

For our purposes, here is my adaptation:

> *"Have nothing on you or your horse, or in your barn or tack trunk, that you do not know to be useful or believe to be beautiful... and hopefully both."*

The first priority for any barn is maintaining a safe environment for horses and riders. Keeping things organized and in their place helps on a day-to-day basis, especially when things go awry. I have had both modest and fancy barns take my breath away with the outstanding organization, cleanliness, purposefulness, balance, energy, and beauty of everything about the place. Horses are large and messy on so many levels, so having a safe, functional, and aesthetically pleasing barn is an accomplishment. As you consider acquiring all the "stuff" you will need, it will be appreciated by any barn if you try to be a positive addition to their environment.

Consider Function, Tradition, Fashion, Aesthetic, and Budget

Before I delve into the extensive list of items you may need, I will share several factors you might consider throughout this shopping process. It is natural to want to fit in when you are a newcomer. But you may not understand how to buy something that serves a function, while also satisfying other potential considerations.

This sounds abstract, so I'll start with a simple example of a halter for a horse.* Most everyone agrees a halter of some sort is necessary. That is, if you want to easily lead a horse, have him stand for grooming in the cross-ties, or catch him in turnout when he prefers to stay out all day, you'll need a halter (for you horse whisperers reading this who can do all these things without a halter, please permit me this example for our newcomers).

Aside from those functional uses, everything about the halter is up for grabs, and you should think about it in order to buy one you will be happy to use for a long time. And so, we consider, in addition to the "function" of the halter, the "tradition" that applies to your chosen horse discipline, what may currently be in or out of "fashion," your own personal "aesthetic," and the vital element of "budget," encompassing both purchase price and how long the item can be expected to last.

As you peruse this table, remember the point is not to spend hours thinking about a halter. Instead, this illustration helps you realize every purchase you make has many considerations. If you are thoughtful about each item on your list, you have a better chance of buying things you like that will serve your needs for a long time.

---

* If you are not familiar with halters, use your favorite search engine on "horse halter" and look at the images to see many beautiful horse heads with halters on them. Even if you know what a halter is, do the search anyway, and you'll see a wide variety of types. You might even add "English," "Western show," "shipping," or any other random horse world variable to the search, and it will give you a sense of what is coming when I describe "tradition."

HALTER		
Considerations	**Description**	**Key Questions** *These questions are illustrative, and likely a bit overkill, for "just" a halter:*
Function	Generally accepted use or uses.	• What is the purpose and use (in our example, a halter helps manage a horse's movement)? • Is there a safety element within function (perhaps breakaway in this example)? • Where will the halter be used (inside, outside, washing, shipping, showing, and so on)? • How long will it be outside, and in what type of elements (on the horse, hanging on a fence, tossed on the ground, in long snowy winters, in long steamy summers)? • How long should it last over time? (The right answer in the case of a halter is, "Years!")
Tradition	What your discipline believes is a "good" or the "best" version of the item.	• What is the most common type in your selected discipline when just buying one halter? • What different kinds of halters do people tend to have if money is no object? • What material, material color, and metal color, for just one or for multiple kinds? (For example, a standard combination for a halter might be leather/brown/brass.) • Is there a name plate? If so, which name (registered or barn or both) is on it? In which font, with the plate itself in which metal color? • Does the barn prefer or require anything specific, including when going to a show? • Will you be shunned by your chosen discipline or barn if you pick the wrong style and color?

HALTER		
Considerations	**Description**	**Key Questions** *These questions are illustrative, and likely a bit overkill, for "just" a halter:*
Fashion	What is "in" right now in terms of type and style, and potentially also brand.	• Is the latest trend to have "silver" or "brass" metal on halters and lead ropes? • Will you be shunned from horsey high society if your horse has a nylon halter when everyone else's has a leather one? Or if your lead rope doesn't match your halter? (Most adults couldn't care less, but for your child rider wanting to make a smooth entry into this world, the "wrong" type of halter could be a thing.) • Are people buying halters from the makers of their saddles to "match"? (This is linked heavily to whether everyone in your barn has a saddle from a certain maker, and how much their self-worth is derived from matching others in the barn or someone famous on social media.) • Is fancy stitching and/or bling in or out now? If in, how much is "just right"?
Aesthetic	Your personal preference as to what you believe is beautiful.	• What types, styles, and colors do you believe simply look beautiful? If those conflict with the tradition and fashion as you know them, which takes priority? • What types, styles, and colors look good on your horse? (Though timeless choices look good on most horses, keep in mind your horse of whatever color is the one wearing the halter in this case.) • How do you want it to look with the rest of your, and your horse's, gear? (Picking a black leather halter with silver trim pieces when all your other leather tack is brown with brass may not be a great call.)

HALTER CONTINUED		
Considerations	**Description**	**Key Questions** *These questions are illustrative, and likely a bit overkill, for "just" a halter:*
Aesthetic (continued)	Your personal preference as to what you believe is beautiful.	• What is your favorite color? Do you like your barn colors? (Beware of buying everything to match your barn colors, and thus making changing barns more expensive. Also, if you just love hot pink and you want to buy as much as possible in hot pink, I say go for it…just make sure you believe you will like hot pink for years, and also ask your barn if they have rules about colors at shows.)
Budget	What you decide to budget after researching the general price range and the estimated longevity of the item (is this something you buy every month, every year, or every few years?)	• First rule: take a hand-me-down that is close enough in type, style, and color before spending money. Most barns and people have crates of old gear, including halters, that just need to be cleaned up and typically can be useful for years. • Aside from the first rule, you can spend what you like and keep it functional. A $20 halter will work; so will a $200 one. If your discipline requires a show halter (a real show halter, as in you lead your horse in one to show him off and it has sterling rather than stainless on it, not just one you want to look fancy in your barn when you go to a show), the numbers go on up from there.

This framework applies to nearly everything you will buy for you and your horse. Buying a new bucket for your horse seems like an innocuous decision. But you can get it wrong and end up having to buy another, so it is worth a similar—if abbreviated—thought process. And though you may presume there are no "fashion" elements to consider with a bucket, there are certainly enough choices in size, shape, material, hook mechanism, color, and so on to make it complicated.

More Gear for You

The section starting on page 52 introduced the "gear for you" needed to get started; this is the "more" (or perhaps it should be "infinite") "gear for you" section. As horses become a passion for you (how could they not?), do your best to retain the key principle from that earlier section: borrow what you can, seek and be grateful for hand-me-downs, hunt in consignment shops (in person if you're lucky, or online), and go for function over form (sometimes the famous brands are worth it, but often you can find something equally functional and even beautiful elsewhere).

Additionally, I would argue that well-maintained, quality traditional items (even if not necessarily in fancy or in fashion) will always be viewed positively. Decking yourself or your child out in the latest, most expensive gear is fine if it doesn't a) detract from your financial ability to do right by your horse in terms of their care, and/or, b) make you (and permit my bit of snobbery here) look excessively "posey" (that is, you appear to be "posing" for the part you do not yet embody—you are "all hat and no cattle," as the saying goes for the wannabe cowboy).

Please remember: you do not need to buy every item on this list right away, or, in many cases, ever.

Cost Description	Low	High
Gear for you—the original list, per the section on page 53		
Breeches	$40	$600
Boots	$50	$1000
Chaps	$50	$500
Helmet	$50	$900
Safety vest	$100	$900
Special shirts	$25 each	$300 each
Special underwear, socks, and belt	$10 each	$200 each
Tack trunk	$100	$1000

Cost Description	Low	High
Gear for you—the "more"		
More of everything in the list above	$$	$$$$
Hairnets (and cute ribbons if desired)	$3	$50
Gloves	$15	$100
Sun-shirts	$30	$300
Sunglasses	$20	$300
Helmet sun brims (very handy)	$25	$75
Show jackets	$50	$900
Vests and jackets (for warmth)	$30	$400
Vests and jackets (to look badass)	$200	$900
Paddock boots	$50	$600
Half chaps	$50	$400
Full chaps (depending on discipline)	$50	$500
Special bags (boot, jacket, and so on)	$30	$300
Boot cleaner, polish, brushes, and rags	$10	$50
Tack cleaner and conditioner	$10	$50
Hat cleaner (especially if you sweat a lot)	$10	$30
A vast array of unrequired yet fabulous horse things with horses or horse paraphernalia on them, including but not limited to: clothes, jewelry, hats, prints, furniture, pillows, art, sculptures, and so on	Small $	Infinite $

More Gear for Your Horse

The section starting on page 49 introduced the "gear for your horse" needed to get started. As part of your education process, obtain one or more hard-copy equestrian supply catalogs (ones that show everything, or at least every category of item, you might buy for your horse). Put it on your bedside table and peruse it regularly. Read the descriptions to get a sense of the following: a) there are many different types of everything (blankets, bits, brushes, and so on); b) there can be a massive price range for each of these items for no apparently obvious reason; and most importantly, c) you should ask for help (from your trainer, barn, horsey friends, etc.) before making any selections, or you risk wasting money on items that are unnecessary, not fit for their purpose (for your horse and you), or simply not well made.

Personally, the most complex part of these decisions is the balance of tradition, aesthetics, and budget. Your riding discipline will have an accepted tradition for how your horse should be turned out. In some disciplines, you will need to follow this tradition when you're showing (for example, a bright pink saddle pad and matching pink polos in the hunter ring are verboten). In others, you may benefit from a bit more freedom (that same saddle pad will not get you kicked out of the jumper ring, at least not until you are up to a certain level).

Cost Description	Low	High
Gear for your horse—the original list, per the section on page 50		
Halters and leads	$20	$500
Blankets and sheets, fly sheets and masks	$50	$600
Boots and wraps	$50/pair	$300/pair
Bridles and headstalls	$75	$2000
Reins and bits	$50	$1000
Saddles	$300	$9000
Saddle pads and half pads	$30	$500
Stirrups and stirrup leathers	$50	$500
Girths and girth covers	$25	$500
Training gear (lunge, etc.)	$50	$500

Develop Your Horse and Your Riding

All the humans and equines involved in this sport progress (one way or another) over time. There is a saying in the horse world that every time you ride or exercise a horse, you are either training him or untraining him. I believe the same applies to riders. You are either consciously refining and improving your skills and habits or unconsciously going backward in your horsemanship and riding.

Everyone seems to understand this point when riding in a lesson. But it also applies when going for a casual ride. For such a ride, you still need to ensure you and your horse are safe, and you need to think about what you are asking your horse to do and stick with a plan so you don't confuse him.

I consider refining my listening and intuiting skills in relation to my horse a beautiful, never-ending journey. Horses talk to us all the time, and it is our gift to learn how to listen, endeavor to understand, and constructively respond. Similarly, our own bodies talk to us all the time, and paying attention helps us (especially those of us getting on in years) stay safe and fit.

Training and Exercise for Your Horse

Especially as a newcomer, it is important to have a better horseperson, likely your trainer, work with your horse on a periodic basis. Even a "schoolmaster" horse should have a professional set of eyes, pair of hands, and (potentially) butt on him regularly. This may involve lungeing, riding, or basic groundwork to address any brewing unhelpful behaviors. In essence, whatever your horse needs. With my own schoolmaster types, I love to have weekly professional contact.

When I had less time to ride and thus had to pay for more professional training rides for my horse, both my horse and I benefited. My horse was worked in a way that used his body more correctly than I was capable of producing, and I could show up to a finely tuned, happy, and responsive horse. The following quote is a text I sent to trainers upon returning from a trip and having a joyous ride on my horse at the time.

"Nothing better than a sound, fit, and happy horse finely tuned and prepared by world-class professionals. In other words...G was great today. Thank you."

Here are some of the things you might expect:

- **Schooling:** This is typically a professional riding your horse for whatever development is needed. That could be practicing your discipline at the level your horse will compete next. It could also be proper work to address any fitness, balance, or rideability challenges. Again, it is whatever your horse needs that you and your trainer have discussed.
- **Lungeing:** Your horse may have fitness needs that are best addressed with professional lungeing, perhaps with corresponding lungeing aids (which is to say, different gear to work on different kinds of fitness). This is not to be over-used (as in the poor horses who are lunged excessively at 5 am in preparation for a show that day), but it can be very productive.
- **Hand Walking:** This may sound like a small item, and it is indeed rare for this to be a problem, but it is quite important. If the horse behaves badly when being hand-walked, that can lead to dangerous situations, especially if he is for your child. A professional should both help to train the horse, and then also train all humans to properly work with the horse to ensure bad behaviors don't return.[*]
- **Other Groundwork:** As with bad behaviors while being hand-walked, any unhelpful or dangerous behaviors while in turnout, being groomed, and so on should be addressed by a professional.

---

[*] If you have ever engaged a dog trainer, you know that only a small part of the process is training the dog. The rest of the effort is required to ensure that any humans who interact with the dog engage in a clear, consistent, firm, and kind manner. Animals are incredibly responsive to our cues, and if a horse senses that you either don't know how to engage properly or are afraid to do so, many of them will take advantage of the situation.

Gear for Training and Exercise

This is not a large section, but you should know that you may need to procure certain gear that will help with the training of your horse. Most often the barn will have basic equipment, but as it is a bit of an art to pick the right gear, don't be surprised if there are some things specifically required for your horse.

- **Lungeing Gear:** The baseline includes an appropriately long lunge line and typically a whip (note the long lunge whip is not for whipping, it is for giving remote signals to your horse).

- **Bridles and Bits:** To me, selecting this gear is both science and art. As a newcomer, you will defer to your trainer on what is the best (humane and effective) combination. And know that bits can be expensive, let alone the bridles. Most barns I have been to have bit boxes filled with bits that might have served a purpose at one time and have been collecting dust since. If they let you borrow one, take a picture of it so you can remember which one—because they all look alike to you at this stage—and put a reminder in your phone to give it back when they ask you for it or you are done with it, whichever comes first.

- **Training Systems:** There are several commercially available systems used to help your horse work better when being lunged, and sometimes when ridden. I have my favorites, but am hardly qualified as an expert on the topic, so I suggest you work with your trainer and read some of the reference books on the topic in the Resources section starting on page 260.

- **Riding Aids for You:** When you can use them properly without hurting, scaring, or bothering (in the wrong way) your horse, you may add some aids to your own gear (crop, spurs, and so on). Only add these items when your trainer says you are ready, tells you what kind you are allowed to use, and then instructs you actively on their use.

The costs of these items range so widely that I haven't included one of my simple tables here. Just know that you should be able to borrow what you need in the early days, but should also be prepared to buy special gear at some point.

Lessons for You with Your Horse

Earlier, on page 54, I included the table below to give you a sense of potential costs for lessons. I repeat it here and add schooling costs to help you build a comprehensive estimate. There is also a spreadsheet available on my website (www. andreasinner.com) that allows you to enter the costs quoted by your barn with your own estimate of frequency.

- **Lessons and Schooling (billed individually):** There will be prices per lesson, schooling ride, hack, lunge, hand walk, and so on. Essentially, any interaction with your horse.
- **Lessons and Schooling (billed in packages):** This is just a different way of billing; it includes a certain number of lessons for you and training for your horse.

Lesson Category	Potential Cost
Private lesson	$50–200/hour
Group lesson	$40–100/hour
Lesson package (discount for multiple purchased at once)	(some barns offer this)
Clinics (outside trainers)	$100–1000/day
Specialized coaching (outside trainers)	$75–500/hour

You may also be presented with options for "training plans." This approach means you pay a set amount each month for a certain number of lessons (or lessons and rides). This is easy to manage, though it is helpful to keep track of everything offline to ensure you are using your full allocation. These are types of models you might see:

- Full training—around 5 days a week of lessons or schooling.
- Partial training—around 2–3 days a week of lessons or schooling.

Cover Regular and Exceptional Horse Care

Board

There are several different models for board. The range of prices you will find varies widely based on geography, discipline, facilities, amenities, and general fanciness. As a broad range, you should not be surprised to be looking at somewhere around $700–2500 and beyond for regular board (which does not include training or lessons). There are far more expensive options as well, but if you're a newcomer in that category of spend, hopefully you have hired an advisor for the process and made sure you are being presented with the standard rates.

- **Dry Stall:** This gets you a stall in the barn, and an allocation of time your horse can use available turnout. You just must do everything yourself (buying bedding, feed, supplements, hay, and general medical supplies; mucking stalls; feeding, giving hay, and filling water; turning out; grooming; and so on). If you are a true newcomer, this is not a good model for you.
- **Regular Board:** This includes "Dry Stall" plus bedding, feeding, regular feed (not special feed or supplements), hay, mucking, water, and turnout.
- **Full Care:** This includes everything in "Regular Board," plus your horse being groomed and tacked up when you arrive, and then untacked and taken care of properly when you're done riding.

- **Full Care and Training:** This is the "everything" model...one set number for full care and all the training and schooling you might ever need. You may still have to pay extra for exceptional medical care or treatments. And you may have to pay extra when you go to a show, but not always. Some trainers and barns just pick a flat number for everything.

When you are looking at a barn, you should ask for their price sheet and figure out what is included in each level of board (if indeed they offer different levels). They may have options for stalls inside, stalls inside with connected runs (a beautiful model if you can find it), runs outside, and a pasture with a shed. Many barns will not offer "dry stall," and as a newcomer you aren't really qualified yet. But they should have options for regular board and potentially full care (where they groom and tack up your horse for you). One side note: as a newcomer, you should have someone supervising your grooming and tacking until you and your trainer are comfortable that you know what you're doing.

Again...Running a Barn Is Expensive and Unpredictable

Here, I am building on the contents of the section starting on page 56. When you consider a barn's expenses just to keep the horses safe and the lights on, what at first sounds like a lot of money for board starts to feel like a bargain. Consider these categories of expenses: real estate mortgage and taxes; building and property maintenance (including trash and snow removal); arena maintenance (including jump purchases and maintenance, if applicable); all employee expenses; property and liability insurance; utilities (electricity, gas, water, sewer); supplies (hay, feed, shavings, and so on); equipment (tractors, mowers, water trucks, and more); manure removal (yes, it's a separate thing); fly management (also a thing); and more.

It is also helpful to remember that board arrangements are usually month-to-month. This means that if you decide to go somewhere else, the barn will be out that monthly income, and sometimes with very little notice (though after reading this book, you will be as polite as possible and give lots of notice). Or if someone else at the barn decides to leave with their three horses, the barn takes a significant surprise hit to cash flow. There are thousands of barns all over the world managing all this, so clearly it can be done. Just know that it is complex and expensive to run a safe, clean, orderly, and good-energy barn.

Farrier

A good farrier is worth every penny. That whole "no foot, no horse" thing is real. Buy yourself a cheap pair of breeches rather than the top-brand expensive kind, but do not scrimp on your farrier. This is another cost that varies so widely by geography it almost seems dangerous to put in price ranges here, but I'm doing it anyway. Just do your research and find the best you can.

Farrier Work Type (assuming all 4 feet per category)	Potential Cost (+ on up)
Trim (no shoes, just a trim)	$50–100
Regular shoes (nothing special, no pads, no extras)	$100–$600
Specialty shoes (special shoes, pads, whatever is needed)	$200–$1000

You should know that your farrier will typically be shoeing your horse every 4 to 5 weeks. Some people have it done every 3 weeks and others (with the right horse, when it is safe for them) can stretch it longer than 5 weeks. Yes, there are horses with Mustang blood that don't need shoes or even a trim as a general matter, but for the rest of us with horses that need shoes regularly…just know you may be buying your horse what I refer to as "a new set of Jimmy Choos" every few weeks.

Veterinarians (General, Soundness, Specialist, Surgeon...)

This is one section where I will not include a range of potential costs. There are some standards and I have a lot of data, but things change regularly and the ranges are even wider than the expansive ranges I presented above for farriers. The best approach is to do your own research with the list below so you can plan financially for both the normal and exceptional costs. The section starting on page 106 includes a discussion of medical insurance to help you when surprise events come your way.

- Regular checkup.
- Soundness assessment.
- Diagnostic testing.
- Vaccinations.
- Worming/fecal check.
- Non-emergency treatments—general health, soundness.
- Emergency treatments—illness, trauma.

Other Medical Care (Dentist, Chiro, Acupuncture, Massage...)

As in the preceding section, there is some volatility in costs for "Other Medical Care" providers. I've included cost ranges to give you a sense, but you should do your own research in your local area to ensure you have an accurate view.

Other Medical Cost Category	Potential Cost
Dentist (regular float)	$100–250
Chiropractor	$100–$400
Acupuncture	$100–$250
Massage	$50–$200

Special Feed and Supplements

The cost of regular feed, whatever your barn uses, is typically covered in regular board. The cost of special feed and supplements, and especially the supplements, is frequently a surprise. If you have a regular protocol of just a few supplements, you can easily spend $50–250 per month. When you get into the high-end supplements, there really is no limit to the potential cost (it can far exceed the top end of that range). I have excluded a table here because there are just too many options, but I will share a few principles for how I look at supplements:

- Work to understand the source of the problem you are trying to resolve with a feed or supplement change, instead of just treating the symptom.
- When changing feed or adding supplements, give them time to work and understand when or if you can stop giving them.
- Try not to change too many things at once, or you'll never understand what helped and what was a waste of money.
- Look at every ingredient in everything you feed your horse, in part to understand if you are doubling up on certain ingredients that may be risky (please ask your vet for help with this one).
- For complex cases, engage your veterinarian and a professional nutritionist to talk about the plan.
- Please don't add a supplement simply because another horse in the barn did well on it or—much worse—your favorite top rider recommended it on social media. Please always check with your trainer and vet.
- Check your sources and the costs—make sure the ingredients are high quality and the costs are reasonable given the market.
- Periodically review and cull the supplements you are giving as not all of them are a lifetime commitment.
- If you are showing, you must know which supplements (and medications) are allowed. Ask your trainer and vet.

Show and Compete

You may have no interest in showing anytime soon, or perhaps ever. That is a perfectly reasonable, and perhaps saner, choice on many levels. And yet, for many people, the love of horses also includes the love of horse sport. If you think you might be interested in the public competitive element, understanding the potential costs is a good idea.

After a few years of riding, I started to budget for two shows a year. As the years went by, my number of shows grew, but I have never had a desire to show dozens of weeks a year. Friends of mine would show that much if horses and money (and time) were no object—note that to show a lot, you will need more than one horse to carry the workload. Understanding the financial costs will help you understand where you want to be in the spectrum of showing frequency.

Cost Variables and Categories

As there are many levels of shows, defining cost ranges is almost impossible and they do change regularly. The following three show variables will have a large impact on your total cost:

- Show rating.
- Show duration.
- Show location (whether it is a local or away show).

An un-rated one-day local show is a great way to get show experience for relatively little money. An "A" show for three weeks in a different state is also great experience, but requires a ton more money. Starting predominantly with the former and moving up to the latter is a sensible approach. Regardless, you need to ensure you have a full picture of the following costs before you sign up:

- Deadlines and deposits.
- Show fees and "splits" (your stall, office fee, class or division fees, shared stalls, and so on).
- Shipping, training, and grooming (showing, coaching, day care, braiding, and so on).
- Tips and gifts.
- Personal travel.

Deadlines and Deposits

All barns will have a deadline by which you must commit to going to the show; this deadline aligns with the show's deadlines. Even small local shows need to be able to plan their numbers to ensure they are set up to provide a positive experience for the participants. Committing early and sticking with your plan is always appreciated.

Most barns also require a deposit to make sure you are serious and to cover costs they will still incur if you cancel after the deadline. Even if your barn doesn't require a deposit, take your commitment seriously. See the sections starting on pages 228 and 230 on being a good barn member and honoring your commitments; it is more enjoyable for everyone involved to be part of a well-organized barn at the show.

Show Fees and "Splits"

This category covers almost everything that will show up on your bill from the show (as opposed to the bill from your barn). The following items describe the show fees for your participation:

- Stall (for your horse).
- Office and association fees (these are shocking when you see them the first time, but they are here to stay).
- Hay and shavings (if you did not bring them from home; typically you will have brought feed or buy it there from a separate source).

- Division or class fees (the actual cost for the classes or divisions, which is a set of classes, in which you are entered).

Costs that are shared amongst everyone showing are frequently called "splits." These costs are commonly split by the number of horses (for example, if you have two horses you will pay twice as much as someone with one horse at the show). However, some barns will allocate some costs by rider, regardless of how many horses each rider has at the show. Some of the costs show up on the bill from the show, while others show up on the bill from your barn. Just know that the show is only doing what your barn tells them to do, so better to ask your barn about any of this rather than fight with the show office.

Pro Tip: To further emphasize that last point, my recommendation is to *never* fight with the show office. They are fine people doing a difficult task while dealing with lots of personalities. You have a right to go politely ask for a justified correction to be made. You do not have a right to act like the person in the office you are talking to did this to you on purpose to ruin your day.

Splits are something which can seem vague and lead to surprises. Accordingly, you should feel free to ask in advance how to budget for the items likely to show up on the bill from the show:

- **Shared grooming stall(s):** Used for grooming all the horses throughout the day.
- **Shared dressing or tack stall(s):** Often one or more stalls for riders to change, store tack and gear, and so on.

Equally important, ask about those costs likely to show up on the bill from your barn, including the three areas I've listed at the top of the next page:

- **Trainer travel, housing, and meals:** This applies to all the professionals going to the show (trainers, assistant trainers, and so on).
- **Groom travel, housing, and meals:** This may or may not be included in the grooming "day care" number, so ask in advance.
- **Golf cart rental:** This might show up on the show bill or on the bill from your barn, and might not show up at all…but know it could be coming, as it is not inexpensive.

Shipping, Training, and Grooming

In your early days, it is unlikely you will be doing your own shipping. In fact, unless you have special skills in this arena, please do not. Assuming your horse travels with other horses from the barn, it may be via a commercial shipper or your barn's truck and trailer. The rate for shipping your horse used to be a nice dependable $1 per mile. As of 2023, it is easily $2 per mile or even higher (due to fuel costs and other general increases). There are also times when you might pay a lot more—for a short haul with a fixed amount rather than cost per mile or if only a couple horses are going. Your barn will do their best to avoid anything excessive; just make sure you understand the estimated costs before you set out on your adventure.

Training costs depend on the price sheet at your barn, but you should be clear before you go to a show as there are widely varying approaches to how to charge. As mentioned previously, some barns with a "full training" plan may not charge you anything additional when you're at the show (admittedly those may be the barns charging you more for full training), while others will charge for every contact they have with your horse and you at the show. Do your homework and make sure you understand how the following items are billed:

- **Schooling:** Trainer or assistant trainer riding your horse to prep him for you.
- **Showing:** Trainer or assistant trainer showing your horse for you.

- **Coaching:** Trainer or assistant trainer coaching you through your warmup, watching your class, and debriefing after.

Grooming will be an additional cost unless you plan to do all your own grooming. While your horse is at the show, he needs the same care and treatment he would have at home; it typically requires a different configuration of, and often additional, staff. Do the math and be prepared for the following items:

- Day care: Most barns offer a "day care" model for care and grooming when at the shows. They may offer it excluding grooming, so just ask. But when your horse is at the show, he needs his stall cleaned throughout the day; he needs his normal meals, hay, and water; and he needs to be ready for each class.
- Braiding: If you compete in a discipline that requires that your horse is braided (mane or mane and tail) and you don't know how to do it well yourself, make sure you know that a) braiders are worth what they charge, b) you will likely get fresh braids for each day you show, and c) it is reasonable but not cheap.
- Turnout or hand-walking: This is a category you will not typically see on bills (because people don't ask for it), but it matters for the health and mood of your horse, so I've included it here. If there are turnouts available at the show, you, or someone you pay, will need to be there to watch your horse. If there are no turnouts, you, or someone you pay, should make time to hand-walk your horse at least once a day (and preferably multiple times).

Tips and Gifts

"Tips" apply predominantly to the grooms taking care of your horse at a show. Calculating a tip as 10–20% of the "day care" fee can be a reasonable approach (note that this estimate is per horse). But ask your trainer and ask other clients what is appropriate (or indeed customary at that barn). Tip in cash whenever possible. Be generous whenever possible and deserved.

Beyond the show grooming tips, there are varied patterns of giving "gifts" during the year and especially during the holidays for just about anyone involved with your horses. The gifts might be cash, gift cards, something you think they would like, or homemade baked goods (for those so inclined and skilled). They might go to your trainer, barn manager, other staff, and so on. Some barns will organize a collection to be split amongst the various staff members; this can be helpful, but it is up to you.

Over the years, I have found cash or gift cards to be the most well-received. I have also periodically given a cash gift in July just because once a year doesn't seem often enough. Whether these are tips or gifts, who knows. Though some trainers and other members of your horse care team make a decent living, the sad truth is the vast majority of people caring for horses do not. Surprise them with a tip or a gift if you can afford to do so.

In addition to all that, say thank you. All the time. Gratitude is free and meaningful.

Personal Travel

Everything above focuses on taking care of your horse. If you plan to attend an away show, you also need to think about your own travel. The costs include the following:

- Getting to the away location, whether by flying or driving.
- Getting around once you are there—using the car you drove there, renting a car, or deciding to rely on friends and ride-share services.
- Having a place to stay, including choosing an apartment, house, or hotel room, and understanding the implications for your meals… If you don't have a kitchen where you are staying, eating every meal out for a long show can be a bit of a drag in addition to being expensive.
- Planning for other pets. Horse people often travel with their dogs; if this is you, make sure everything above takes your canine(s) into account,

and know that most horse shows require dogs to be on a leash, if not in a restricted space, anytime they are at the show.

In addition, you need to think about how much time you can take off from work or school and away from your responsibilities at home for these adventures in horse showing. If it's the summer or you are totally flexible, great stuff. For everyone else, make sure you use your holiday, vacation, and other time off judiciously.

Legal Considerations

In many areas of our lives we have legal considerations we tend not to think very much about. We generally try to obey the law, pay attention when we sign a contract (though typically without reading the fine print), and perhaps buy insurance to manage known financial risks. But mainly we trust that going with the flow will keep us out of trouble. Though there are unique considerations in the horse world, most people continue to operate in the same way.

Though it is slightly risky, I certainly went many years in my horse journey before understanding the potential legal complexities or contemplating hiring a lawyer. We would all rather spend time with horses, or at least be thinking about how to find the right horse or barn, than contemplate our legal health. However, a bit of energy spent on the additional legal considerations brought about by joining the horse world frequently saves time and money in the long run.

What Is "Legal Health"?

When contemplating a life well-lived, I consider my "health" across the following categories: physical, mental, emotional, occupational, environmental, social, communal, spiritual, existential, financial, and legal. It is likely because I am a lawyer (my second career) that I think "legal health" deserves its own category rather than being a subset of financial health (though they are often intertwined).

I define "legal health" as being aware of, compliant with, and protected to the greatest degree possible in all the legal respects that impact me and my family, friends, animals, and assets.

Being aware means I understand not only my legal responsibilities (for example, knowing I am liable for my horse's actions), but also where the law is a helpful tool (contract law exists for good reason, but you really need to write everything down). Being compliant means upholding my responsibilities to avoid running afoul of the government (for example, having my horse's Coggins test result certificate when he ships across state lines) or other individuals (for example, paying my bills and complying with executed contract terms on time). Being protected means using legal instruments to alleviate or soften negative impacts when things go wrong (for example, adding a provision in a horse purchase and sale agreement to clarify exactly when the risk of loss transfers between parties, or buying major medical insurance for my horse when I know I couldn't afford an emergency colic surgery bill).

I hope this section gets you thinking about the legal considerations new to you as you join the horse world. For anyone interested in exploring the concept of legal health promotion, along with dispute avoidance, dispute containment, and dispute resolution—all considered within access to justice—I highly recommend Richard Susskind's *Online Courts and the Future of Justice* (published in late 2019, a couple months before the pandemic). Where Mr. Susskind is prescient, I am nascent.

Your New Legal Responsibilities and Risks

Almost everything you do has a legal element that is unlikely to be self-evident—again, just like most aspects of our lives, including when we sign on to the terms and conditions for online apps and memberships. To illustrate this point, here are some of the topics that may soon be relevant to you:

- **Liability and insurance:** This includes equine activity liability laws, releasing liability, horse owner liability, horse mortality and major medical insurance, and more.

- **Contracts and agreements:** This includes contracts and agreements arranging training, leasing, boarding, buying, shipping, co-owning, and so on.
- **Compliance and regulations:** This covers topics such as government regulations regarding shipping; equestrian governing body rules regarding registration, horse and rider safety equipment, horse and human behavior, horse medications and vaccinations, competition; and more.
- **Estate planning:** This includes how all your equine-related affairs will be handled at incapacity and death, and is vital when you own one or more horses to ensure they are cared for properly through their natural lives when they—to put it bluntly—live longer than you.
- **Liens and debt recovery:** a.k.a., you didn't pay someone what you owe them—whether it's a stable, veterinarian, farrier, or other service provider lien; general contractual debt recovery; or something else.
- **Negligence and malpractice:** a.k.a., you have an issue with someone's service—again, this could apply to any of the various service providers.

Over time, you should endeavor to understand your state's laws and regulations for everything above. Someday—likely not in your early days with horses, but eventually—you may also need to understand other legal aspects of the horse world such as importing, exporting, quarantining, breeding, syndicating, horse property ownership, and equine business ownership, to name a few.

The reason I'm not telling you to do all your homework immediately is because your barn should know about all these things. To give you a sense of how complicated it is, when you are engaged with horses in the United States, your barn must be conscious of the laws, regulations, and rules of the following entities and more: U.S. Department of Agriculture (USDA), Federal Trade Commission (FTC), Internal Revenue Service (IRS), state law (for regulations governing equine activity liability, equine activity safety, equine fraud, contracts, dispute resolution, probates and trusts, and more), one or more state Departments of Agriculture, one or more state Veterinary Boards, United States Equestrian Federation (USEF), Fédération Equestre Internationale (FEI), any breed-specific associations, any discipline-specific associations, and more.

For anyone interested in learning about the equine industry's legal elements beyond what this short section provides, I highly recommend Julie Fershtman's *Equine Law and Horse Sense*, published by the American Bar Association and with over three hundred pages on this vital topic. She has been a lawyer for over thirty years and has written more than four hundred articles on equine law. Where Ms. Fershtman is a legend, I am a newbie.

STORY

Pet Trusts Are a Thing, and Detailed Care Instructions Are Vital

Over fifteen years ago—well before I became a lawyer and focused on estate planning—I began to worry about what would happen to my horses should I suddenly die. How would ownership transfer, and to whom? Would they continue to be treated in the way I wanted them to be? Who would be able to pay the not-inexpensive bills for them? Who would ensure they were cared for their entire natural lives and be treated with dignity in their final days?

And so, I found myself an attorney to help me "put my affairs in order." Taking care of the four-leggeds in my life, in addition to the two-leggeds, was important to me. Today, all states have on the books some form of the concept of a "Pet Trust." This is a legal instrument that allows you to allocate money for the care of your animals, define who will be the caretaker, and define who will manage the money. Importantly, because a Pet Trust works like a revocable living trust, it will be valid if you become incapacitated, in addition to after your death.

Though the two roles in a pet trust could be filled by the same person, most states allow them to be filled by different people. Just as you consider designating guardians for your children in a will, you might have one person who is well suited to bring your children into their home and raise them, while another person, who is better with money, fills the job of making sure the funds you left are used—and stretched over time—in all the ways you had in mind when you executed your estate planning documents.

Over the years, I have refined my pet trust to have much more detail about how I wanted my horses treated, and also expanded my list of backup caregivers and money handlers. Just as I have done with my own health care proxy designees, I make sure everyone has agreed to the role and knows where they are in the sequence. My caregiver designee for a certain horse may be ready to serve today, but life circumstances change and so they should feel comfortable politely deferring to the successor caregiver if needed.

Obtain Independent Counsel for Contracts and Important Documents You Sign

Nothing in this book replaces talking with an attorney—optimally, an experienced equine attorney. Here is my short pitch as to why it is worth the time and money to talk with an attorney:

- **You don't know *what* you don't know.** This book is designed to help you know more, but it only has so many pages, and you are still new. I've been in the horse world for twenty-five years and a licensed attorney for seven years, and yet I still learned many profoundly simple things when attending a recent Equine Law Conference. This area of law is vast, complex, and changes every day. Nothing replaces experience when considering the risks and permutations of things that could go wrong.

- **You don't know *who* you think you know.** After following the barn search process described in this book, you decide to work with equine professionals you respect and like. And then you trust their opinions about who they respect and like. And on down the line. Even with good intentions everywhere, the childhood game of "telephone" teaches us multi-party communication is dicey. Add the potential for one or more bad actors (or just that one tiny fib or omission of detail) to the mix, and you are exposed. There isn't enough paper in the world to protect you from all potential poor outcomes, but when humans are involved, it's best to clarify more rather than less.

One Omitted Detail Can Put Horse and Rider at Risk

STORY

Years ago, I was reasonably diligent when buying a lovely mare (multiple trials, full pre-purchase exam, and so on). The first few weeks with her were as fabulous as we hoped they would be. And then, what seemed like suddenly, she stopped at a few fences (small cross-rails, to be clear), and off I came. We stopped jumping and did only light hacks, as she seemed happy with that, and tried to figure out the problem.

About a week later, she went into heat. In a big way. What we subsequently learned, and what the seller had decided not to tell us when sharing how to care for her, was they had previously had her on multiple (not just one) medications to prevent her cycles in an effort to make her more comfortable, quieter, and easier to work around. There are many opinions on these types of medications, and I will not delve into that here. What was objectively egregious was transitioning her care to us with no mention of it.

Did the seller exclude this vital information on purpose because they were worried it would sour the deal? Who knows. But whether intentional or ignorant, the net effects of this omission were: 1) that poor mare was forced off a substantive amount of medication cold-turkey, which was both dangerous and unfair, 2) I was hurt in my fall, but luckily physically it was only some bruises that went away quickly, and 3) I lost my riding mojo for many months and engaged a sport psychologist to get it back (see page 236 for that story).

And so…even with a bunch of people who trusted each other between buyer and seller…*you don't know **who** you think you know.*

As you might guess, one of the reasons for my detailed Horse Transition Template, which includes medications, is to force a detailed conversation. We thought we had handled it all verbally when we transitioned this particular mare's care, but maybe the checklist would have helped.

- **Experienced attorneys can be engaged simply for simple transactions.** We have an access-to-justice problem worldwide, and the United States is no exception. Part of the problem, particularly in the United States, is the cost to become an attorney drives up the costs to hire an attorney (note I said "part" of the problem…if you're interested in this topic, feel free to reach out to discuss it further). But if you start small—for example, help with a simple in-barn lease agreement—you may be able to find an attorney for just that small engagement. Don't presume any call to an attorney will break the bank.

- **Having an attorney who knows you when something goes wrong is valuable.** Part of the reason I suggest starting small is to give you a chance at building a quality client-counselor relationship over time. If you decide you do not like the attorney you hired, you can remedy that hiring mistake when the stakes are low. And when you find the right advisor and engage with them periodically over the years, they will know you and be there for you if something big goes wrong.

If You Ignore That Advice, Still Take It Seriously

If I have not been sufficiently persuasive and you still want to proceed unassisted, I hope you consider the following ideas about taking it seriously.

- **Do your own independent research.** Search engines and artificial intelligence can be helpful, if still a bit dangerous because you have no experience to help you sense-check what you are reading.
- **Talk with others who have done something similar.** Whether it's a simple liability release or a complex co-ownership agreement, ask for lessons learned and example documents, even if you can only get them with some parts redacted.
- **Brainstorm your objectives, deal breakers, and concerns before you read any draft documents.** As a newcomer, once you look at a draft of any document provided by your barn or another party, your reaction will probably be, "Wow, that's an impressively long document…it must be comprehensive!" But likely it is neither complete nor fully supportive of your interests. Doing your own thinking in advance helps you spot errors and gaps when you look at a draft.
- **Read anything you are asked to sign in detail.** Print it out and read it again. Ask questions about anything you do not understand. And, critically, ask if you can make changes. For a liability release, the answer is likely, "No," and so your options are to sign and ride, or go someplace else; for a purchase and sale agreement, however, the answer should be, "Possibly, depending on the change."
- **Keep track of everything you have agreed to.** Record your agreed-upon responsibilities in whatever way you will remember them best. For example, if there are terms like, "lessee must inform lessor if they wish to continue the lease two months before the term of this agreement ends," then add a calendar reminder that gives you a chance of complying with this term. Save the final document—preferably the one signed

by all parties—in multiple places; keep a hard copy in your files, save a digital version on both your laptop and your phone, and so on. Make sure you or another party has emailed that same final version to everyone involved.

Write. It. Down.

In addition to hiring an attorney and taking it seriously, one final simple message: write it down. Whether "it" is your preferences and instructions, an agreement with another party, your commitments, a purchase and sale agreement, or anything else, everything is easier to manage when you write it down. Some suggestions:

- **Document health care decision rights in case you are unreachable.** You must be explicit about what your barn is authorized to do—and authorized to arrange with a veterinarian or equine hospital to have done—on your behalf for your horse. The last thing you want is for your horse to be sick or hurt, with you unreachable and nobody authorized to give him the care he needs (this happens, and it's on you for this error, not your barn's staff, who will stand there helpless and in tears without the authorization to do right by your horse). Write it down, show it to everyone who needs to know, post it in your trunk, and email it to everyone for good measure.

- **Notify your horse care team of insurance protocols.** If you have insurance on your horse, the insurance company will have rules about notification of injury or illness—and you are typically accountable for contacting the actual insurance company, not your agent. Read all the rules in fine print and take them seriously, as they can make the difference between being covered or declined. Likely, you will be the one to call the insurance company, but these events are stressful, and it's best if multiple people know the exact notification requirements.

- **Formally document any purchase and sale agreement, bill of sale, lease, and so on.** These may seem easy to handle, but verbal deals can lead to confusion and conflict later. Document them, review them in detail multiple times, and make sure all involved sign them.

Seek Advice about the Different Types of Insurance Available

If you have read this section about legal considerations, then you understand why insurance for the new risks in your life might make sense. There are many options for insurance when you get involved with horses. Typically you will consider such options when you lease or buy a horse. For a lease, the policy holder will likely be the horse's owner, but you should know the terms and your notification responsibilities as discussed above.

The decision to buy insurance for and related to your horse is complex. You need to consider your appetite for risk, ability to pay for major medical expenses that may come up, ability to recover from a full loss of the horse's value (in case of an unexpected death), and ability to handle costs associated with any injury or damage your horse might cause. Here are some questions to ask yourself:

- If your horse dies a year after you buy him, can you afford to buy another horse if you don't have his value insured?
- Are you comfortable paying 10 years of insurance premiums only to never make a claim?
- Can you roll the dice by not having any medical or surgery insurance and having to suddenly pay out-of-pocket for colic surgery?
- Are you comfortable with the ever-increasing cost of the insurance as your horse gets into the age range when you will more likely need coverage?
- If you didn't buy medical and surgical insurance and your horse needs (costly but not astronomical) surgery you cannot readily afford, are you comfortable taking out an emergency loan to cover it?

Having thought through those questions as a horse owner, you are better prepared to talk with a licensed equine insurance broker about the following types of coverage:

- **Mortality and Theft:** Full or partial value of the horse.
- **Loss of Use:** Typically partial value of the horse when he can no longer do his intended job (tread carefully with this one).
- **Medical and Surgical:** Typically for major medical, surgical, and colic-specific surgical.
- **Private Horse Owner Liability:** For situations in which your horse causes injury or property damage.
- **Air Transit:** Specific coverage if you are transporting a horse by plane… yes, that's a thing.

Do the Math and Make Informed Decisions

Doing the math in advance is fundamental to not getting extended so far that you risk your horse's physical health, your own financial health, or both. Every horse person I know has at one time or another spent more than they originally intended. Even with great intentions, I have done the same myself. And even when I have thought things through, I have spent more than was likely a good idea at the time. For example, I took out a loan against my 401k to purchase my first horse in the late 1990s. This is not a good financial strategy in general, let alone for something arguably optional. So, know that these creatures can inspire reckless financial behavior.

Define and Review Your Budget on Different Time Horizons

Complete a Multi-Year Analysis

First, do the math at a multi-year level. One exercise I went through just a few years into my riding was to estimate my horse spending over the coming decade, add a reasonable amount of interest if I were to invest that money rather than spend it on horses, and then stare at the resulting number. Any number across ten years with interest added becomes a bigger number. Even though the number took me by surprise, I ended up being comfortable deciding that I would rather have my experience with horses than that number in my savings account at the end of the decade. That choice led to many tradeoffs, but I have never doubted it was right for me. Please make sure it is the right one for you.

Conduct a Formal "Annual Review"

Second, do the math at an annual level. Everyone's circumstances change periodically, and it is better to adapt as early as possible rather than let things go too far. You must adjust if you know your income is going down or other expenses are going up in the coming year. If you hoped your horse would last you another three to five years and instead it looks like you will need to a) retire him in a year (if he has simply reached that age and physical status) or b) sell him (if he is still able to do a job and you want to go bigger or faster or whatever it is), think ahead to how you will be able to handle the shift. Remember, until a horse is sold, you cannot count on that money; consider his price a sunk cost and see the section starting on page 65 about the ever-present risk of needing to retire a horse earlier than planned and having those expenses across many years.

Spot-Check Your Spending Periodically as Well

Third, do the math within each year as frequently as you can stomach. I once spent so much on a young horse, essentially an investment and ridden by professionals, that I started limiting the showing I was doing myself with my primary horse. If I had done the math earlier, I would have started the process to sell the young horse earlier; but I only caught it at my annual review. So instead, I limited my riding progression because I hadn't thought it all through well enough. I recognize this sounds like a fancy problem (#FirstWorldProblems), and it is. But here is another common example: You decide to attend one more show than you originally budgeted, and you end up without enough money for normal medical care for your horse (let alone unplanned medical costs).

One of the key themes of this book is to only go as far with horses as you can while still taking quality care of the one(s) for whom you are responsible. If you don't have the time to pay attention to your horse, but have plenty of money, you can pay people to pick up your slack. But if you don't have the money to fulfill your responsibilities, the horse will eventually pay the price. Whether you have <$500 a month or >$500,000 per year available, there is a horsey plan available for you…and when you get your math right, you can be confident you are in a reasonable position to do right by the horses in your life. So, please: do the math, add 10–20 percent of contingency to that math, make informed decisions, and take the best care possible of the equine athlete(s) in your life.

Diligently Manage Your Budget and Work to Save Money

Unless you like to overpay (or you have more money than time), do know there are ways to manage and save money in the horse world. Here are some thoughts on how to help yourself in the journey. Each of these have helped me at different stages.

- **Find an equine accountability partner.** This could be your significant other, but often not. Essentially, you commit to explaining any variance from your annual or monthly budget to this person *before** you spend the

---

* Clearly the point is to talk about things in advance. However, if you get swept away in the moment, either by committing to or actually spending the money, call your accountability partner anyway. You can debrief what happened, talk about what it means to your overall budget, and (perhaps, if you're feeling brave) discuss how you might avoid the transgression the next time.

extra money. Their job is not to give you permission or withhold it. Their job is to remind you of your budget and everything *you told them* about why you needed to stay within that budget. Simply explaining yourself to someone you respect and trust in this role can sometimes be sobering enough. And sometimes, you decide to spend the money anyway, but feel better because you are doing so with eyes wide open.

- **Set up a horse bank account.** Putting your horse-designated money in one account is a helpful way to ensure you are sticking to your budget. Use it for your Venmo/Zelle transactions—since, finally, in the horse world, almost nobody uses checks anymore—and get a debit card for anything where you need a card. You get the point here. When the account is empty, you don't get to buy that expensive monogrammed blanket for your horse that he doesn't need anyway. When the account is close to empty, you can decline the next away show. Tracking your horse money other ways can get to the same outcome, but this is an easy and highly visible way to do it.

- **Maintain a detailed budget.** The more detail you have in your budget, the easier it will be to know what makes the cut and what doesn't. It's like going to Target with a shopping list instead of just going for a bit of a wander. The former gives you a fighting chance of getting out of there having spent within your means. The latter almost surely leads to overspending by two or even three times.

- **Be more planful.** Planning ahead helps in everything. If you are headed to a show, do any needed shopping in advance. Make a detailed packing list so you don't forget things. The alternative is "last-minute buys" at the show, where you will likely spend more (it's like buying your protein bar at the airport for $6, compared to at your local grocer for $2). Being planful applies to everything. If your barn has a full truck of horses headed to the show, your shipper can take that into account. If you get your entries in on time, you don't have to pay late fees (and likely won't have to pay more for your own travel).

- **Manage pounds and pennies.** Building off your detailed budget, watch where the money is going. The big-ticket items—a horse lease or purchase, where you decide to have your horse and ride, how many and which shows to do—matter, of course. Yet keeping track of a zillion modestly priced items also matters.

- **Find other sources.** For anything you might be thinking about spending money on, think about whether you are going for the "easy shiny new" or trying to find a reasonable deal. There is no excuse for overpaying on general merchandise when you can search vendors online. And that includes places offering "gently used" items that may serve your purposes for years to come. You can also buy in bulk for many things in the horse world. Talk with your horse friends and do some research; you can likely save around the edges.

As with every section of this book, you can find more about this topic online. Craft your online searches using the chapter and section titles from this book, your chosen equestrian discipline, and your geography.

Chapter Four

Find the Right Barn—One Willing to Support Your Riding Dreams

Knowing Nothing, I Still Found a Magical Place to Start My Horse Journey

As noted in the introduction, I decided to start riding when I was thirty years old. At the time, I was based in Virginia and yet, given my consulting lifestyle, was working each week in Houston. I looked in the Yellow Pages (which were a thing in 1997) and called several places.

I found a wonderful horsewoman who taught both English and Western, and, importantly, welcomed beginners. I don't remember many other riders. I do remember her teaching me one-on-one, everything from getting my horse in from the pasture, through grooming and tacking up, and then slowly finding enough comfort in the saddle to walk, trot, and canter. This was one of those places built for the safety and comfort of horses. Not fancy, but, at least to my eyes and senses, a wonderful place for horses to call home.

Eventually, my aspirations and a bit more disposable income led me to find another barn that was focused on the hunter discipline. I had a wonderful conversation with that first trainer explaining that I wanted to make a shift. Her maturity and professionalism seemed all quite natural. There was no drama—in coming years, I would learn how rare her response to my changing barns locally had been. She had done her part to get me started and was excited I was going to continue my journey with horses.

That first trainer reminded me of the mother of the family that had allowed me to ride their pony Zingo for a couple weeks in Vermont, two decades prior. Their love of horses, deep expertise, ability to teach, attention to detail, and direct nature were all a gift to me. That very positive experience in Houston set the stage for the years to come, and I remain grateful for it.

The Professionalism and Energy of a Barn Matter in Equal Measure

Much of this chapter is dedicated to the elements of selecting a barn that you can judge objectively. This includes the facts and your basic perception of the facility, the competence of the people on staff, and the age and riding level of other boarders and riders. This chapter also endeavors to elicit your feel of the place. That includes the energy of the environment inside and outside, how people interact with each other, and what the horses tell you about what life is like there.

Selecting where you want to ride, and potentially to keep a horse if you have one, is a massively important exercise. Unless there is a world-class facility with reasonable prices, great horses, and good friends ten minutes down the road, you will likely be making tradeoffs. This chapter has frameworks and questions to help you think through the complex exercise of making the decision—use the checklists and templates, or scan them to get the gist. Many questions are designed to bring out how you feel about the place.

How you allocate your thinking time on this topic is up to you. My hope is that you will spend quality time reflecting on the energy of your possible places to ride. A fancy barn that checks almost all the objective boxes but has an undercurrent of superficiality, elitism, and shaming is likely not the best place to start your riding journey—especially if it is your child's riding journey. A less fancy barn where camaraderie and caring for each other and the horses is evident is typically better when you are very new to the horse world. There are, of course, fancy barns with great camaraderie and caring, and there are less-fancy barns with nasty trainers, horrible rider cliques, and constant barn drama. My point is that the energy of the place is important. So, take the time to reflect.

I start to measure the energy of the barn from the moment I see the place when driving up. It continues as I get a sense of the aesthetic of the entire place—how I feel when I get out of the car, what the dogs do (meaning the dogs already at the barn—do not bring your own without asking), how the horses appear and react to what is going on around them, whether the bustle of barn life seems to flow or is frenetic, how people interact with each other, and how people interact with me. You are choosing a home, and one that should be a source of great joy, warmth, fulfillment, connection, development, and community. Choose wisely, using both your brain and your heart.

Evaluate Multiple Barns and Trainers

If you have made it this far in this book, you are beyond the stage of only going on trail rides while on vacation. You want to learn horsemanship, learn how to ride, and potentially get your own horse.

Assuming you are indeed ready to go further, this is one of the most important sections of this book. Especially in your early days of riding, how you feel about the people, horses, and program at your barn matters. How the humans—both barn staff and your riding peers—treat you as a newcomer can bring you into the fold or send you running. The horses they have for you to ride, and how good the trainers are at matching you with a horse, set the stage for your horse journey. How the barn treats all horses, and especially yours if you get one, impacts your overall experience. And the general approach and program at the barn will either help build your competence and confidence, or, in a less positive environment, perhaps leave you feeling inferior and frustrated.

This is a *very* serious decision. You are putting yourself in a position to engage with these people a great deal, and the professionals in the barn are the authority figures on many topics—even though you may be very accomplished outside the horse world, it's different here.

In the sub-sections below, I share many areas you could consider as you determine whether you might want to engage with a particular barn. I include a Barn Evaluation Template starting on page 134, which includes (literally) one hundred suggested questions. The template is designed to be used repeatedly as needed, so not every question—especially those that presume you have your own horse—will apply in your first barn search. It is fine if you don't want to fill out the template in detail. Just remember: it is easy to get swept away by a barn when you meet a couple of cool people and, for example, love the lesson horse they say would be great for you. And though your gut feeling is massively important (and, indeed, is included as a category in the template), using a bit of rigor helps you make sure you are investing your time and money wisely. Even if you have a best friend at a prospective barn and really want to go there, going through this evaluation process will help you go into that barn with eyes wide open.

Barn Type and Culture

Barns range in size, clientele, and showing frequency. A big barn that shows more than thirty weeks a year and requires all clients to show a certain number of weeks per year is one model. A smaller barn with optional showing just a few weeks a year is another. And any barn, big or small, that doesn't show at all is yet another beautiful model. If a barn is run well by experienced people who care deeply about horses, every single model within this wide range can work well. It's all about matching the feel, environment, and program that works best for you and, if you have one, your horse.

Additionally, every barn has a unique culture, level of professionalism, and way of working. There may be a single person (trainer, barn owner) who sets the tone, or it may be a couple of people (married couple, business partners, siblings), or even several people (consider a family-run business, or just good horse people who have worked together for a long time). Though not always directly correlated with overall culture, the pricing at a barn also influences who is attracted to the barn and how many amenities are available.

EVALUATING BARN TYPE AND CULTURE

- **Leadership:** Who sets the tone for the place? Is it one person or more and what are they like?

- **Size:** Just a few horses? A medium barn of 20 or 30 horses? A big barn of over 40 horses?

- **Client age:** Mostly kids or juniors? A nice blend? Mostly adults?

- **Client experience level:** Mostly newbies? A nice blend? Mostly experienced?

- **Horse ownership:** Some lesson horses? All horses privately owned?

- **Showing level:** Limited, if any, showing? Medium level of showing? Constant showing?

- **Pricing:** Inexpensive with no minimums? Modest rates? Higher rates with more amenities?

- **Board and care offerings:** Dry stall only? Regular board? Full care options?

- **Stalls and turnout:** Basic stalls with sand turnout? Sizeable stalls with reasonable grass paddocks for a couple of hours per day? Massive stalls in a beautiful structure with fabulous large grass paddocks for several to unlimited hours per day? Stalls with runs, along with available grass paddocks, for the best of both worlds?

- **Amenities:** Just the basics? Nicer ring(s)? Nicer tack rooms/kitchen/showers/ whatever else, too?

Frequently, You Don't Know What You Don't Know

Early in my horse journey, when I leased my first horse, I rode at a barn with an unusual profile of offerings. In many ways, it was a fancy barn. There was a clubhouse with a kitchen and a patio for parties (and there were parties!), an air-conditioned bathroom to shower and change, decent tack rooms with everyone having matching trunks (that's a thing in some places), several good rings, and a modest cross-country course. However, there were also almost two hundred stalls and no grass turnout. As it was my first barn, I didn't think much about it (everyone else seemed to think it was okay for their horses to have sand turnouts for a small chunk of time each day).

Then a colleague at work said our new CFO, coming from another location, had a wife with several horses. They were interested in where I rode, and I shared the details. When the CFO later joined our team, I learned that his wife had liked my barn, but chose a location farther outside the city where her horses would have daily grass turnout. Today, my permanent barn must have good turnout; even when we are at a show for a couple of weeks, I dislike the typical lack of turnout. On reflection, that time was still wonderful. The horses were healthy, and I could ride in the mornings before working in the city each day. But my values have changed, and these days, quality grass turnout is a must-have for me.

The point of this story is that many circumstances can work well, and some work well at different times in your life. It is up to you to be clear on your values and make the best decision you can. Most places will not have everything you want, but if you're clear on your deal breakers, you will find something that works.

Trainer Relationship

Most barns have a single trainer or a team of trainers with some type of hierarchy (perhaps a single lead trainer with assistants, or two lead trainers with or without assistants). A larger facility might have multiple trainer teams, each being its own business and typically having a unique name. Finding the right individual trainer or trainer team as part of your barn search is vital; if your "favorite" barn doesn't have a trainer that works for your level, showing desires, and budget, it's simply not a good match.

The Barn Evaluation Template starting on page 134 includes several questions to consider in relation to trainer fit. Often, as a newcomer, you will be working primarily with an assistant trainer; this is fine, and sometimes even better, as a more senior trainer might not have the patience you need in the early days. But if this is the case, you need to meet the assistant trainer to ensure you feel like you can take lessons from this person. This is another area where references are important; talk with someone of your age (or someone of your child's age and their parent) regarding their newcomer lesson experience.

EVALUATING TRAINER RELATIONSHIP

Do they have a reputation for:

- Running a professional, friendly, and low-drama barn (you can have all this while also being a highly competitive barn, which you may or may not want)?
- Giving effective, and hopefully fun, lessons?
- Keeping an excellent and qualified staff (for every role)?
- Managing respectful positive relationships with horse and property service providers?

Do they have a track record of:

- Finding good horse matches for clients, especially newcomers (this is such a talent when you find it)?
- Helping clients achieve their riding and competition goals?

For variables where any approach can work, does their model feel good to you:

- Training team size—One-trainer barn? A couple of trainers? A full team with a hierarchy?

- Showing aspirations—Stay-at-home trainers? Show-all-the-time trainers? A blend of both?

- Social style—Separation between barn time and social time? Periodic social activities? A committed social director?

Evaluation Approach

You may already have a barn in mind, or you may be using your favorite search engine to explore your area. If it is the latter, take your time and talk to lots of barns and people; visit lots of barns; don't commit too early; and take lessons everywhere they have lesson horses (some barns do not, so see below on the difference). There is no better way to get a feel for a barn than by going there, taking lessons, and spending time watching and learning. And even if you find a place is not quite for you, they will almost always be able to point you someplace that might be better for you.

Evaluation Categories

The categories of questions in the Barn Evaluation Template (starting on page 134) include the following:

- Potential deal breakers for newcomers.
- Pricing.
- Trainer relationship.
- Horse care team.
- Barn basics.

- Culture.
- Gut feel.

Evaluation Steps

Note that if you sit down with a barn owner or trainer to go through all the questions in the Barn Evaluation Template in a first meeting, their eyes will likely glaze over (there are 100 questions!). That doesn't mean you can't do it, but I suggest you follow these steps:

1. **Narrow down your deal breakers.** Make a list of the criteria which are a minimum for you. This list should be very short. Peruse the Barn Evaluation Template starting on page 134, initially focusing on the aptly titled, "Potential Deal Breakers for Newcomers."

2. **Visit the barn's website.** Review the barn's website for all the basics and a general feel. Please note that many barns are not great at keeping their websites up to date, but most will have something out there. Do them the favor of having read everything before you make your first phone call, even if that call is just to confirm something that might be a deal breaker.

3. **Make some phone calls.** Call the barn owner or trainer to review the "Potential Deal Breakers for Newcomers" in the Barn Evaluation Template starting on page 134 with any potential barn. If the barn doesn't have lesson horses and you don't have your own horse, you don't want to waste your time or theirs going through the remainder of the template. But *do* ask them who (barn or specific trainer, or both) they would recommend for someone in your newcomer status—and why.

4. **Determine your criteria.** After learning a lot from your phone calls, read the full Barn Evaluation Template. Reflect on the template and develop

your own perspective on which are the most important questions to have answered (maybe have a piece of paper with your top questions, or photocopy the template and use a highlighter to mark them).

5. **Visit and listen.** For any barn you have a good feeling about or a positive reference for that has passed the "potential deal breakers" section, schedule a time to meet with the barn owner(s), trainer(s), or both. Allow them to describe the barn in their own words, and to share further details as they give you a tour.

6. **Ask questions.** During that meeting and tour, ask any questions that come to mind. Also ask to talk with other barn staff and clients. If possible, watch a lesson with people at about your (or your child's) level, as that will be very informative.

7. **Take multiple lessons.** Even if you love everyone at the prospective barn and their reputation is excellent, you still need to see if you have chemistry in the trainer-rider relationship in lessons. One or two may not be enough to know for sure, but it is a great start.

8. **Assess using the template criteria.** If you think any barn is a contender, and you like being methodical (it is completely fine if you don't!), fill out the template.

9. **Summarize your evaluations of the top contenders.** If you end up with two or more barns as contenders, list your top three positives and top three negatives about each barn. Reflect on those and, assuming no deal breakers are amongst them, use the "gut feel" questions as your tie breaker.

Understand How Your Barn and Trainer Run Their Business

In the sections starting on page 56 and 87, I shared a bit about most businesses in the horse world working to make ends meet. This may seem like an odd section to revisit here, but trust me: it helps to understand just a bit about how your barn runs their business. It will save you from being frustrated by things that don't seem logical when they likely are (for example, having to pay up front for certain things when you would normally expect to have 30-60 days to pay). It will also make you kinder and more diligent in being a good client—you will understand how to be a client that helps make things better rather than being a constant drag on operations and cash flow.

When you begin your horse journey, you will be regularly surprised by the size and frequency of the money you are regularly sending various businesses to support your habit. It starts simply enough with paying for a few lessons on a lesson horse. It balloons quickly when you lease or buy a horse, and perhaps add showing into your plans. All those costs are outlined in Chapter 3 starting on page 47.

The point of this section is to get across that most barns, independent of commissions when they can recover ground sometimes, are making very little, and in some cases, zero money. Every horse business—barns included—must hire and retain quality, experienced staff; keep up to date with a vast number of suppliers; pay for their own facilities, utilities, and insurance; handle normal and abnormal (read: COVID, weather) expensive surprises; and try to collect from people who love horses yet often struggle themselves to make ends meet.

As discussed throughout this book, you have a responsibility to extend yourself into the horse world only as far as you can reasonably afford. When you follow this principle, you can pay your bills (both the expected and the unexpected) on time and help the whole system move along better. Your barn, trainer, vet, farrier, and other professionals are responsible for delivering a quality service at a reasonable price. They are not responsible for giving you a break and serving effectively as a bank by holding your unpaid debts. You are responsible for paying your bills on time.

I do not share this perspective to get you to feel sorry for people in the horse business. Most of them get to work with the animals they love doing a job they love, and indeed they presumably chose their path. I am also not ignoring that a small minority of horse professionals swindle their clients to make more money than would rightfully come their way (it happens, as discussed in the section starting on page 56).

However, the vast majority are in this game for the love of horses, and the math generally doesn't work in their favor. That is why you see many amateurs with fancier breeches than their trainers. Keep an eye on what you spend and how transparent and fair everyone is being, but also please do the horse industry a favor and hold up your end of the ecosystem by meeting your financial commitments.

Know That Your Barn and Trainer Do Not Own You

These Relationships Are Complex and Intertwined

Your relationships with the trainer and other key professionals in your barn are multi-faceted. I can think of no other set of relationships that has the blend of roles I describe in the chart on the next page...

For whom:	Roles your professionals may play:
You	• Service provider—you are paying them for a set of services. • Coach—and all that entails…educator, psychologist, mentor. • Safety advisor—your life is in their hands, in many ways. • Financial advisor—for all things horse-related. • Travel companion—where applicable. • Friend (see the section on page 231 about choices here).
Your child	• Coach—and all that entails…educator, psychologist, mentor. • Safety advisor—as the parent, you are relying on the professionals to guide your child in this dangerous sport. • Nanny—depending on their age.* • Travel companion—where age-appropriate. • Idol—this is not unusual.
Your horse	• Caretaker and advocate—a massive, massive job. • Aunt or uncle—don't forget, they love horses too.

---

*   See the section starting on page 232 regarding watching out for minors in the horse world. That section also introduces SafeSport in the United States, which was authorized by Congress and has rules and guidance related to minors in all sports, including equestrian sports.

Similarly, you play a blend of roles for the professionals:

For whom:	Roles you may play:
Barn owner	• Paying client. • Member of their barn community. • Friend.
Trainer (may or may not also be barn owner)	• Paying client. • Student. • Member of their training community. • Visible example of their work (how you act and generally progress with horses reflects on their reputation, even if you don't show or compete). • Friend.
Barn staff	• Member of the group of people in their work environment. • Friend.

Barns Do Not Take Everyone Who Knocks on Their Door

When a barn and trainer take you on as a client, it is not a simple decision. They must consider your personality, objectives, and constraints when determining whether you will blend in well with their business and their other clients. They must also consider your horse, if you have one already, or what you need for a horse to ride if you do not. Do not presume that all barns want any new paying client, and that they should simply feel lucky to have you. Barns want good clients that will be a net positive across all dynamics, not just anyone with some disposable income.

After they welcome you into their barn, they invest in you to integrate you into their community and work hard to support you, and perhaps your child, to achieve your objectives. They spend far more time thinking about you and how to do that than you might guess. Developing a good barn where people get along well, are progressing in the sport with healthy happy horses, and there is limited "barn drama" is bloody hard work.

All that backdrop is important to understand why, beyond the obvious financial incentives, barns and trainers are protective of their business and clients. That is natural, and, I think, a fine thing when it incentivizes them to continue to deliver exceptional client service. When you are in such environments, revel in it, and do everything you can to reciprocate by being an exceptional client (see the section starting on page 228 on being a good barn member).

And Yet...Watch for Signs That They Think They Own You

Where this goes off the rails is when your barn or trainer(s) start to believe they own you. If you've been in the horse world for a while, you will already understand this dynamic (if not from your own experience, then from hearing stories). But for the newcomer, it is mind-boggling. How can a service provider believe they have a right to control a client spending a reasonable, let alone hefty, amount of money for said service? And what would that even look like? So here is what that could look like:

- **Happy days at the start:** Rarely will a situation feel uncomfortable or weird at the beginning. It is all so new; you're just letting it wash over you.
- **Growing dependence:** Initially, you *are* dependent because you don't know anything. But if you are willing to do the work, you should be able to grow these relationships to the point where you are reliant and yet not over-dependent on your professionals. "Reliant" meaning you collaborate constructively with your team—to be clear, I cannot do a good job taking care of my horses without my entire team of amazing professionals, but I am not beholden to them until the end of time. "Over-dependent" would mean your trainer and team make all the decisions and you do as you are told.

- **Unable to question:** Unless you ask the same question several times (which means you're not paying attention or doing the work to grow your horsemanship), you should always feel comfortable asking about anything related to your horse's care, your riding, your progression in this sport, and all of the related finances. My experience is that a problem in this arena is the first indicator of a dysfunctional relationship: something doesn't make sense to you, but you don't want to "offend" whichever professional is involved by questioning them. Your friends and family will often notice this before you do…when you start getting sensible questions from them like, "That seems wrong. Why can't you just raise that issue with your trainer?" or "You have asked them for that multiple times and you are the one paying the bills—why can't you put your foot down?", then try to nip it in the bud, or at least make a note to watch for further bad behavior.

- **Isolation:** You have a right to have lovely horse-related conversations with anyone you like. Should you be airing your latest complaint about your barn, when you haven't even bothered to raise it *with* your barn? My view is a hard, "No." Be an adult, be respectful, and talk with your barn first. However, if you just want to chat with a rider from another barn, great. If you want to talk with another trainer, great as well. If you are simply chatting with clients or professionals at another barn and your barn blows a gasket, this is an indicator that they may not be terribly evolved as humans, and you need to be on alert for further bad behavior.

- **Gaslighting:** This term is over-used in public discourse at the moment, but it's the right one. The point of gaslighting, in this scenario, is to get you to question your perception of reality, question the validity of your thoughts and reasoning, and ultimately increase your dependence on and deference to the professional. The tactics involved can include telling outright lies, retelling stories in modified ways, denying any wrongdoing, using other people to support their view of the world, and many others. If you are typically a confident and competent human being and you begin to regularly question your judgment and memory, find a trusted friend to share the situation with to discern where you may indeed be off and where you are being gaslit.

- **Financial captivity:** There are degrees to this one, but the worst (quite rare) would be a professional having massive control of how you spend money and prioritizing their own financial, reputational, or personal priorities over yours. A unique element of this one is that it is often you, the amateur, who starts the ball rolling. You love your trainer, want to see them succeed, and are magnanimous and generous. And then somewhere along the way, you realize your own objectives (or those of your child) are not being met and you are spending more than intended for the benefit of the trainer.

Special notes for parents of minor riders:

- **Everything above applies:** Your challenging task is to try to protect your child from anything untoward when you aren't there all the time.
- **Potential for abuse:** The section starting on page 232 discusses this important and difficult topic in more detail. The power dynamics are unique in the horse world, in that the professionals hold a power position with your child *and* with the horse that your child holds most dear. That nuance makes it arguably even more difficult, compared to other sports. And as minors, simply because of their age, they rarely have the skills to recognize the beginning stages of different types of abuse.
- **Manipulative triangulation:** This is a fancy term for a professional inserting themselves into the family dynamic in ways more helpful to the professional than to the minor or parents. The professional may convince your child they need to do something that benefits the professional (for example, buy an expensive horse that's really a match for the professional, or go to a series of shows not vital to the child's objectives), and then make you, the parent, the bad guy if you do not agree to it.

Special note for those with a lot of money:

- **Everything above is amplified:** If you have a lot of money, see the section starting on page 254, as everything in the above lists can be amplified by your net worth.

Special note for smart accomplished people:

- **You are not immune.** No matter what you have achieved in life, you are not immune to anything above. Highly intelligent, well-educated, and professional top achievers can and do fall prey to these issues. I have been there myself—in minor ways, luckily—and I have watched many other smart people I respect greatly find themselves there as well. I believe part of the reason for this is that if you have accomplished a great deal in your occupation, you presume horse professionals are operating with a regard for ethical and disciplined practices as high as yours is. The vast majority do—but to protect yourself from those that do not, whether due to incompetence or nefarious intent, you need to use all the skills in your toolkit, and not leave them at the barn door as many before you, including me, have done.

What to Do When You Are in the Wrong Barn for You

This is a delicate topic for all involved. The horse world seems to struggle with the idea that sometimes it just isn't a good match amongst rider, horse, trainer, and barn. With all those parties involved (including the most important one, the non-human one), it is no wonder it can be a potentially fraught collective relationship. You may determine you have the wrong situation for your objectives a few months or a few years into your relationship; regardless of timing, making a transition is never easy.

Story: Know That Old and New Trainers Talk to Each Other

When your current and potential trainers are friendly, the potential new trainer may call the current one for "permission" to take you on. This concept infuriated me the first time I learned of it (how dare they treat me like a piece of meat in the middle to be discussed behind my back), but I hadn't understood the etiquette many trainers follow. Trainers collaborate with other trainers, both at home and away at shows. Their relationships and business can span decades; clients will quite honestly come and go (though they hope most stay), but their peer colleagues will likely stay fairly consistent over the years. It makes sense they do not want any "bad blood." I still dislike that a new trainer might only take me if my current trainer—the one I might be having issues with—gives their okay, but at least I know (and now you do too) this is a likely hurdle.

Story: Know That Old and New Trainers Sometimes Dislike Each Other

Starting note: Bad human behaviors exist and may even be amplified in the horse world. Sometimes barns and trainers dislike each other and can't help but feel a wee bit of satisfaction when they can "steal" clients from each other. It's not the prettiest side of the horse world, but there it is. You should do your research to see if this might be the situation. You have every right to go where you want to go, but if you're opening Pandora's Box, it helps to tread lightly and try not to get caught in the cross-fire.

Make Sure You Have Tried Everything to Make It Work

There are factors that can influence you to stick it out a bit longer in your current situation:

- **Finish the play.** Getting better at riding and improving your horsemanship takes time. If you are in a situation for just a few months and unhappy with your progress, you need to seriously consider whether your expectations are out of whack. Have a reset conversation with your trainer and give it a bit more time.
- **Moving has risks.** The grass often appears greener, but making a transition can be hard on you and, if you have one, your horse. Before you commit to a change, you should rigorously assess whether the things you are unhappy with a) truly can't be fixed in your current barn, and b) are genuinely likely to be substantively better in the new situation.

Stand Firm in Your Values and Priorities, and Make the Move If It Is Merited

There are also factors that are not your problem and should not sway you to stay:

- **You do not need to stay in an unhealthy or unproductive situation.** This statement is as true in life as it is in the horse world. And yet, many barns and trainers are deeply offended if you say you want to leave, and some are known to trash you in the horse world if you do. Their reaction is often a blend of hurt ego, lost business, and a perception of maligned reputation. If you have made your complaints clear and given them a chance to improve things, and nothing has come of it, you do not need to stay for fear of hurting their feelings or making them angry. You may lose some friends in the process (some trainers are known to gossip about you to your peers at the barn and make them pick sides), but—sorry for being trite here—your real friends will know the full story and have your back.

- **You do not need to keep their secret if your barn or trainer has verifiably done something wrong.** Please take the high road and stick to a simple version of the facts when you leave a barn, or perhaps even sugarcoat it a bit if it's just a relationship that came to a natural end. Superfluous and juicy gossip helps nobody. However, if you have verifiable evidence that your horse was mistreated, you were lied to, or you were swindled, a simple version of those facts is reasonable to share with people you know who might benefit from the information.

Handle Your Search for a New Barn Confidentially and Respectfully

A delicate part of this whole process is finding a better situation while, in some cases, not wanting to tip your hand. You will need to talk with another barn or trainer to find a better fit—most likely in advance of giving notice. Some horse professionals may be hunting your business and promising the world; be wary of the big sell and walk away if they gleefully trash your current trainer. Others may be friends with your trainer and inform them that you are looking. As mentioned above, the horse world tends to stick together.

Here are some principles when you are considering new options:

- Clarify your key deal breakers (things you like in your current situation and don't want to lose) and complaints (things you need to have improved).
- Make sure you have given your current barn a chance to address your complaints. Be honest with yourself on this one! Moving barns because you couldn't muster the courage to discuss your complaints is potentially disrupting (read: putting at risk) your horse for no reason and is simply irresponsible behavior. Be an adult and have an adult conversation with your barn and trainer.

- Talk with friends you can trust not to share that you are thinking about moving, and compile a short list of potential barns that you think could meet your needs.
- Follow the same evaluation process in Chapter 4 starting on page 112, with your choice of two approaches:
  - » Attempting to keep your search private. This likely means forgoing taking lessons with potential trainers and limiting your time for visits, as barn staff and clients are prone to chattiness.
  - » Letting your trainer know you are conducting a search. This approach allows you to not stress so much about keeping your search hidden, and to potentially take lessons at the new prospects.
- Make sure each potential barn understands whether your search is private or out in the open, and that regardless you appreciate their discretion and will not make any commitments immediately.

If you need to go through a transition of this kind, do make sure you have a trusted friend to talk things through with you. It is almost always easier said than done, but when the circumstances require a move, you owe it to yourself and your horse to settle in a place better for you both.

Once you have decided to leave, handle it professionally. Unless you are truly worried about your horse's safety—which will be exceedingly rare—you should give reasonable notice, such as one month or longer. You will need this time, and your barn's help, to prepare the Horse Transition Template starting on page 181, which is designed to help you safely transition your perfect equine. You should also use the related instructions 4 and 7, starting on page 174. And when you do move, pay your bills, pack up everything you own—including the old horse blankets they let you store in the attic—and generally leave everything better than you found it.

Templates
Barn Evaluation Template

Barn Name	
Barn Address	
Travel Time to Home	
Travel Time to Work/School	
Primary Vet	
Open Barn for Vet (Okay to use others?)	
Owner(s)	
Trainer(s)	
Barn Manager	
Head Groom	
Primary Farrier	
Open Barn for Farrier (Okay to use others?)	

Category	Question	Answer	Happy with answer?
Potential Deal Breakers for Newcomers	**1.** Do you have lesson horses for newcomers, or do I have to have my own horse?		
	2. What are the barn days and hours of operation? When are lessons typically offered?		
	3. How many other newcomers (people with less than a year of experience riding) are in the barn?		
	4. How many people are in my (or my child's) age bracket a) regardless of riding level? and b) also a newcomer?		
	5. Is there a minimum amount of spending or number of lessons required per month?		
	6. How much should I be prepared to spend for startup costs (for example, gear for me) and ongoing costs (lessons and riding fees) in the first 6-12 months of riding?		
	7. Is showing required at any point in the future? (*Note:* Some barns require that you show a certain amount per year.)		

BARN EVALUATION TEMPLATE CONTINUED

Category	Question	Answer	Happy with answer?
PRICING			
Lessons	**8.** Private lesson, school horse?		
	9. Private lesson, own horse?		
	10. Group lesson, school horse?		
	11. Group lesson, own horse?		
	12. Any packages of lessons?		
	13. Hand walk?		
Exercise	**14.** Lunge?		
	15. Hack by trainer or qualified barn staff?		
	16. Professional schooling by trainer?		
	17. Packages of lessons + other exercise?		
Board	**18.** Regular Board (stall, feed, hay, stall cleaning, turnout)?		
Full Care	**19.** Full Care Board (same as Board, but my horse is groomed, tacked up, and untacked for me each time I ride, and groomed daily regardless of whether I ride him)?		
Medical Care	**20.** Is special medical care (giving medication, applying medication, wrapping) charged?		
Medical Care	**21.** Is handling my horse for any care team visits (vet, farrier, chiropractor, and so on) charged?		
Commissions	**22.** Commission for lease?		
	23. Commission for buying/selling?		

Category	Question	Answer	Happy with answer?
TRAINER RELATIONSHIP			
Selected Trainer	**24.** Which trainer(s) would I primarily be working with?		
	25. If I would be working with an assistant trainer, would I get to take a periodic lesson with the head trainer?		
Lessons	**26.** Would I be primarily in private, semi-private, or group lessons? How much choice do I have?		
	27. Have I been able to take a lesson from the person who would be my primary trainer?		
	28. Have I at least been able to watch the person who would be my primary trainer give a lesson to someone at my level?		
Reputation	Does the head trainer(s) have a reputation for: **29.** Running a professional, friendly, and low-drama barn (you can have all this while also being a highly competitive barn, which you may or may not want)?		
	30. Giving effective, and hopefully fun, lessons?		
	31. Keeping an excellent and qualified staff (for every role)?		
	32. Managing respectful positive relationships with horse and property service providers?		
Track Record	Do they have a good track record of: **33.** Finding good horse matches for clients, especially newcomers?		
	34. Helping clients achieve their riding and competition goals?		
Connection	**35.** Would I be comfortable spending time over coffee with my trainer(s)?		
	36. Would I be comfortable telling my trainer(s) what is working for me in their program, and, importantly, what is not?		

Category	Question	Answer	Happy with answer?
HORSE CARE TEAM			
Barn Staff	**37.** Is there a barn manager (beyond barn owner or head trainer)? How long have they been in this business and worked here?		
	38. How many other staff are typically here each day, and how long have they typically worked here?		
	39. Are there any working students or volunteers?		
Vet	**40.** Who is the barn vet?		
	41. Do you allow other vets of my choosing to come treat my horse? What are the protocols for that (do I need to be there, or will the staff handle those visits)?		
	42. Who are your other key vets (soundness, specialist, and so on)?		
Regular Care	Does your primary vet keep track of the following for all horses? **43.** Vaccinations		
	44. Coggins		
	45. Health certificates		
	46. Worming		
	47. Dental		
	48. Privates cleaning (for both boys and girls!)		
Farrier	**49.** Who is the barn farrier?		
	50. Do you allow other farriers of my choosing? What are the protocols for that (do I need to be there, or will the staff handle those visits)?		
	51. How often does your farrier typically come?		
Commissions	**52.** Commission for buying/selling		

Category	Question	Answer	Happy with answer?
HORSE CARE TEAM			
Other	**53.** Which other care specialists (chiropractor, massage, acupuncture, and so on) are regularly at the barn?		
BARN BASICS			
On Site Support and Protocol	**54.** How many barn staff are typically on site?		
	55. Do any people (barn staff or others) live on the property? Who are they and can they hear the horses overnight?		
	56. Do you have written emergency procedures that everyone is familiar with? Do they cover normal natural events (wind, fire, flood, and so on) and horse incidents (colic, wounds, illness, getting loose, and so on)?		
Stalls	**57.** How many stalls (or runs, or sheds)?		
	58. How many horses (that is, are all horse spaces being used)?		
	59. How big are the stalls? Any with attached runs?		
Rings	**60.** How many outdoor rings are there?		
	61. Is there a covered ring?		
	62. Is there an indoor ring? Is it heated?		
Viewing	**63.** What kind of viewing areas are there for each ring (what kind of seating, covered, HVAC)?		
Paddocks	**64.** How many paddocks? What size?		
	65. How long are horses typically in turnout each day? Is it flexible for horses who like more time outside? How frequently does the weather mean turnout is unavailable and what happens then?		

Category	Question	Answer	Happy with answer?
BARN BASICS			
Exercise	**66.** Is there a treadmill or a hot walker?		
	67. Is there a round pen?		
	68. Any other horse exercise facilities?		
Feeding	**69.** How many times a day do you feed? Give hay?		
	70. What time is night check?		
Groom/Wash	**71.** How many grooming stalls?		
	72. How many wash stalls?		
Tack	**73.** How many tack rooms? Are they temperature-controlled?		
	74. Is there room for my tack trunk (if I have one now or if I get one in the future)? Is that in a temperature-controlled area?		
Kitchen/Bath	**75.** Is there a kitchen or break area?		
	76. How many bathrooms?		
	77. Is there a place where clients can shower?		
CULTURE			
Clientele	**78.** How many clients take lessons on school horses? How many have their own horses?		
	79. How many clients are in each general age bracket (kid, junior, 20s-30s, 40+)?		
	80. Are there casual and impromptu social gatherings at the barn, and what type? Are there planned social events, and what type?		
Showing	**81.** How many clients show regularly? How many generally stay home when others are at the show?		
	82. At shows, do clients typically come to watch other clients compete (support each other)?		

BARN EVALUATION TEMPLATE CONTINUED

Category	Question	Answer	Happy with answer?
SHOWING			
Frequency	**83.** On average: How many local shows per year? Away shows per year? Overall weeks of showing per year? Are there any big shifts for longer periods (going to Florida or another warm horsey place for the winter)?		
	84. On average, how many horses and riders go to each show?		
Home Coverage	**85.** When part of the barn is away at a show, who is available at home to give lessons?		
Pricing	**86.** Is there a separate price sheet for shows?		
	87. How do you handle shared costs or "splits" (grooming stalls, day care, grooming, trainer and staff housing and travel, and so on) for each show?		
GUT FEEL			
Energy	**88.** Before I got out of my car, did I take a few deep breaths, per page 18?		
	89. When I got out of my car, did I feel good about the environment in terms of visuals, sound, smell, and energy?		
	90. Did I feel better in my body when I walked in and around the place, meeting horses and people?		
	91. Did the energy of the barn seem welcoming and relaxed, and yet also serious about taking care of horses and people?		
Horses	**92.** Did all the horses I saw (in stall, turnout, or being ridden) seem happy and relaxed? (Note: A horse or two that looks stressed and puts their ears back is not a reason to disqualify a barn, but if most of them do it, that might be worrisome.)		

BARN EVALUATION TEMPLATE CONTINUED

Category	Question	Answer	Happy with answer?
GUT FEEL			
Staff	**93.** Is there a barn manager (beyond barn owner or head trainer)? How long have they been in this business and worked here?		
	94. How many other staff are typically here each day, and how long have they typically worked here?		
People	**95.** Did I like the people I met, including the owner, trainer, barn manager, grooms, staff, clients, and so on?		
	96. Could I spend time with these people in the barn, in a lesson, or at a show?		
	97. Might I be able to make friends with some of them (riders or parents of young riders)?		
Environment	**98.** Was the barn orderly, clean, and apparently safe to my liking? (Note: You may not require fancy and barns have a range of tidiness, but make sure you feel comfortable in the environment you see.)		
References	**99.** What did other people, ones who can be objective, have to say about this barn, their program, the clients, and the horses?		
	100. If I have a good or best friend in this barn, am I sure that relationship isn't making me ignore some possible deal breakers? (It's okay if you choose a good friend as a way to override some criteria; just do that with eyes wide open.)		

Chapter Five

Discover the Right Horse—One in Your Optimal Ownership Model

The Beauty of Leasing a Horse

Back at the show stalls with the horse who was a candidate for me to lease (this would be my first lease), I thought I heard my name announced. We had just finished a hunter class of some kind—this was too long ago for me to remember—and I had thought I was terrible. So we were both cooling off and generally chillaxing in the shade. It never occurred to me that I should go check how we did.

I had been riding at my current barn for over a year. I loved the school horses, and yet, now a few years into my riding and with my career progressing enough to consider this option—read: I had a few extra \$—I was yearning to have a horse of my own. My trainer was amazing at talking me through the concept of leasing versus owning (I am forever grateful for that). And off we went to hunt for my equine companion. Of the several horses I had tried, this particular horse lived in our barn and was going to a nearby show. I had tried him at home, and the owners were gracious enough to let me take him in a couple classes at the show as a further trial.

I did not have fancy checklists. I had no idea what I was doing. But I had a trainer I believed I could trust, and the decades since have validated that trust. And I was having fun with all of it. When I learned what I had thought was a "terrible" round had earned me a red ribbon, I was hooked on that perfect gelding that had clearly packed me around.

Though I learned that leases can be more expensive and complicated than you might think (see the section starting on page 55), it was a great first step into horse ownership. I leased that brilliant creature for a year, and he taught me so much. Though I moved on to fully own a different horse after him, that first year he gave me was incredibly educational and rewarding.

Staying at a Comfortable Spending Level Helps You and Your Horse

Surprises happen all too frequently when you are engaged with horses. My mantra throughout this book is to help you make sure you have the time, money, and energy to do right by the horses in your life—indeed, I believe an equivalent of this sentence shows up a multitude of times in this book. The focus in this section is primarily on the money side of the story. You need to have a financial cushion for surprises. And perhaps, when they are related to surprise medical costs, insurance to soften the blow of an urgent surgery or treatment. But all that is obvious.

What is not obvious is that if you have leveraged yourself too far, you may start to scrimp on the important regular maintenance your horse needs. These may seem like small decisions, like procrastinating in setting up a dental checkup or not buying more of the hoof supplement your horse needs, but they are vital to the long-term health and wellness of the horse. Most horse people I know take much better care of their horses than they do themselves, but there are some horse people who start making bad choices because they didn't plan well.

In the case of major life events that impact your finances dramatically, the right course of action is to find a different situation for your horse so he does not suffer. Life happens, but if you keep yourself at a very reasonable spending level, you will be able to weather any sudden changes. If that means you volunteer or work around the barn for catch rides, that's fabulous. If it means you save for a couple more years to have a much better cushion before buying a horse, that's great too.

Pre-Ownership Options

There are so many ways to enjoy being with horses before riding them, let alone owning them. Even if you are flexible on funds, I recommend being around horses for as close to free as you can find. Before you start buying gear and paying for lessons, go volunteer somewhere. Before you even consider half-leasing a horse, take as many lessons as you can and offer to help around the barn. Though most people who have an inkling they want to be with horses end up completely enthralled, it is still good to make sure before you invest heavily with your time, energy, and money.

It is also wonderful to see what good people are doing for horses in need, and what horses are doing for people in need. Here is a short list of the many options available to you:

- Volunteer at an equine charitable organization (rescues, sanctuaries, therapeutic riding centers, and more…use your favorite search engine to see what is in your area).
- Go to Pony Club (available mainly for children, but also potentially for adults, depending on your area).
- Take lessons on a school horse. This will cost some $, but is a nice entry-level opportunity.
- Go to a clinic or camp for newcomers. This will also cost some $, but is deeply informative.

Evaluate Multiple Ownership Models

Understanding the range of ownership models available is vital to moderating your commitments (time, energy, money) to match your level of interest and what you can fulfill. Going longer in the "lesson" status than you might want helps you make a better choice for your first half-lease. Starting with a half-lease allows you to test the waters of being responsible for a horse before taking the next step. A full lease (often six or 12 months, potentially with an option to extend or buy) helps you become even more comfortable with your horse and the role you play as the lone partner and advocate for that horse.

Your options include:

- **Half-lease of a school horse:** This helps ensure you work with the same horse for your lessons—that may happen anyway, but this is a way to ensure that.
- **Half-lease of a horse in the barn:** This may allow you to expand to some fancier horses, but know that for your first half-lease you still need a schoolmaster.
- **Full lease of a horse in the barn, or from a different barn:** Another barn will need to trust your barn's ability to care for the horse before they will agree to move him to your barn.
- **Purchase:** You're the new owner, responsible for everything until retirement, sale, or death.
- **Co-ownership:** This is when you decide to go in with someone else on a horse, or pay an existing owner to have some percentage of ownership.

Many barns, trainers, and often friends will push you to skip some of these options. My key point (before we get into the details of these options) is to keep in mind the massive responsibility that comes with full ownership. You are responsible for the horse for the rest of his life. If you move, if he gets sick, if you have a financial crisis, if he turns out to be too much horse for you, if he turns out to be not enough horse for you, or if you just fall out of love with riding, he is still your responsibility.

If he's still a good horse for someone, you might be able to sell him to a good home—always the goal. But if he had a career-ending injury, you may simply have to retire him. A retired horse can cost $250-1500+ per month for basic care (see the section starting on page 65 for more detail on retirement). Horses can live to be thirty years old and older. Please do the math before you buy a horse.

Half-Lease (a.k.a., Split-, Share-, or Partial-Lease)

The simple premise of a half-lease is that you pay part of the expenses to ride the horse part of the time. This is in addition to whatever lease fee you might need to pay, or there might be no lease fee in certain situations (the "free half-lease"). The split of expenses may be a 50/50 (or any other percentage split you agree on) arrangement with someone, or you may pay a set amount to your barn for a certain number of "rides per week" on a lesson horse. There are a massive number of variables you should consider as you decide if a particular "half-lease" opportunity is right for you.

In addition to making sure this is the horse you want to ride (see the section starting on page 159 for those criteria), consider the following:

Who is responsible for the following expenses, and at what percentage of the total?

- Half-lease fee—what is the fee, if any, in addition to the share of the subsequent items in this list?
- Insurance—this is typically bought and paid for by the owner, but the lease may require additional funds to cover it. See the section on page 105 about insurance notification requirements.
- Board.

- Training rides (if needed).
- Vet, farrier, and all other expenses for the full care team.

Who is responsible for the following care duties?
- Coordinating with the care team for vaccinations, farrier visits, soundness checks, and so on.
- Grooming beyond the daily "get tacked up" grooming—this includes bathing, clipping, and so on.

What access will you have to the horse?
- Rides per week—lessons only? Will you be allowed to ride on your own? Note: Please ensure no more than 6 days a week are allocated, as every horse deserves at least one day off.
- Schedule—Which days and times will each person ride? Note: Assign only one person per day. Unless you're only doing short walk/trot lessons, one person per day is the best.
- Showing—is this a possibility? How would the split work for showing?

What are the terms of the arrangement?
- Time commitment—is the half-lease month-to-month, or does it extend for a certain number of months, or something else?
- Notice of cancellation—must you give notice if you do not want to continue your half-lease at the end of the defined term?

What happens in the following circumstances?
- If the horse becomes ill or lame and cannot be ridden for a while (a couple days, a couple weeks, or even a few months), who pays the bills, and what happens to the current half-lease agreement?
- If the other person who rides the horse wants to change their "regular" days, who helps resolve this conflict if the two of you can't reach a new agreement?

- Even though you've agreed that you are each only allowed to jump the horse a certain height (or perform other high-impact work in your discipline) one day a week, you've learned the other person is jumping him higher twice a week, and they think that's totally fine—similarly, who helps resolve this conflict?

Full Lease

A full lease is a big step forward, as you are assuming full responsibility for the horse. In a way, it is simpler than a half-lease because you do not need to negotiate responsibilities and time. But it also means it is all up to you (albeit with support from your barn, trainer, and horse care team).

As with a half-lease, there are many variables you should consider as you decide if a particular "full lease" opportunity is right for you. In addition to making sure this is the horse you want to ride for the foreseeable future (see the section starting on page 159 for those criteria), consider the following:

Who is responsible for the following expenses?

- Lease fee—is there a lease fee? What is the amount? Is it all paid up front?
- Insurance—this is typically bought and paid for by the owner, but the lease may require additional funds to cover it. See the section on page 105 about insurance notification requirements.
- Major medical expenses—if these are not covered by insurance, who pays for them?
- Note: You are likely responsible for every other expense typically associated with owning a horse. As noted in the section starting on page 105, writing all of this down helps.

What happens in the following circumstances?

- What if the horse becomes ill or lame and cannot be ridden for a while in the middle of the lease (for a couple days, a couple weeks, or even a few months)?

- What if the horse dies in the middle of the lease? Yes, this is a terrible thought, and yet it does happen, and it is best to discuss all of these scenarios in advance.
- What if the owner, in the middle of the lease, puts restrictions on how much you can compete and at what level? How do you resolve this, and do you need the respective trainers to facilitate this?
- What if you have an accident (horse-related or otherwise) or become ill, and cannot ride the horse for a large portion of the lease period?
- And any other scenario you can imagine yourself, or can imagine with the support of an experienced attorney (see the section on Legal Considerations starting on page 97).

Full Ownership

In multiple sections of this book, I've cautioned you about the massive step of buying your own horse. It may sound like I don't want you to buy a horse, but that is not true. And, of course, what I want doesn't matter. What I simply and deeply hope is that you only buy a horse when you are ready, willing, and able to be the best horse-mom or horse-dad you can be. I hope you have thought deeply on the topic and are committed to having this horse as an integral part of your life.

Being Thoughtful and Excited for Your Lifelong Partnership

Because a purchase is a simple transaction compared to a lease, your primary considerations are the following:

- Is this the horse you want to care for and ride for the foreseeable future (see the section starting on page 159 for those criteria)?
- Is the age of the horse a good match, keeping in mind there are no guarantees on the working lifespan of any horse?

- Can you afford the purchase price and the commissions, and still handle all the ongoing expenses with a bit of money to spare for contingencies (see the section starting on page 70 for budgeting)?
- Do you have the time, energy, passion, physical energy, emotional bandwidth, and money to fulfill the following roles for this horse with love and rigor:
  - » **Guardian:** You are the CEO of your horse's life.
  - » **Protector:** You will fight to the end of the earth to safeguard your horse.
  - » **Advocate:** You proactively and reactively serve as your horse's voice in this world.
  - » **Champion:** You support your horse in what is best for him, not for you or others.
  - » **Friend:** You know and are sensitive to your horse's needs, behaviors, and moods.
  - » **Partner:** You collaborate with your horse on your shared endeavors.
  - » **Financier:** You, quite simply, pay for everything your horse needs to live a good life.
  - » **Mom or dad:** You demonstrate your love for and commitment to your horse every day.

Simple as pie…have a positive response to everything above and you are ready to be a horse parent!

Co-Ownership

Sharing the time, energy, and financial responsibilities for a horse can be a compelling option in certain situations. However, as with any partnership, the relationships can be complex. Distinct from a half-lease where you can extract yourself from the other humans involved at the end of the lease period (though sadly the horse relationship may go as well), the shared ownership model can be more difficult to alter.

You should consider every question in the section starting on page 147, which describes the half-lease model. In addition to making sure this is the horse you want to ride for the foreseeable future (see the section on page 159 for those criteria), consider the following:

- Do you trust, and believe you can work and resolve issues with, the other co-owner(s)?
- Have you documented, or at least discussed in detail, all the principles for the shared care, training, and riding of the horse?
- Have you agreed on how you will resolve disagreements, both the (sometimes easier) day-to-day ones and the (rarely easy) big gnarly ones?
- Do you know how you will handle it if one of the parties can no longer afford the time or money to be part of the arrangement, or wants to sell their share to someone else?
- What will happen if the horse needs major medical interventions, a period of rehabilitation, or even an early retirement?
- Depending on the extent of the relationship, have you talked with a lawyer about how to properly document the business and horse treatment principles and commitments?

Evaluate Multiple Horses

When you are a newcomer, your qualifications for selecting a horse are hardly sophisticated (you don't know what you don't know). Yet, you must remember that you are in the driver's seat; it is your passion, your potential partnership with a horse, and your money. You should listen to your riding peers—they will have many stories to tell about the horses that did and did not work out for them—but most especially you should listen to your trainer. Your trainer's job is to keep you safe and learning; they should be able to guide you to a match that should serve you well in the coming years. Remember that when you went hunting for a barn and trainer (as discussed in Chapter 4 starting on page 112), part of your criteria was the trainer's proven (via references if necessary) ability to match horses and riders.

And yet, you are buying this horse for you, not for your trainer or any of your riding peers. You might end up moving to a new place in a year or two and all those people will be left behind. You and your horse will carry on together, and it is worth your due diligence to give yourself the best chance at a good match. I use the term "best chance" as there are no certainties in the horse-matching business. You might have great trial rides and everything looks great on paper (the horse's record, his pre-purchase examination report, and so on), but sometimes the relationship isn't the perfect match you thought it would be.

Price

Horse prices range from $0 ("free to a good home"—though sometimes risky, it can also be a beautiful thing) to literally millions. When you start discussing prices with your trainer, and perhaps your friends and riding peers if they will discuss it with you, you will likely be shocked at the numbers. Take a deep breath and review the total budget of owning a horse (see Chapter 3 starting on page 47) to see it all in context. It is an over-simplification, yet fundamentally true, to say that all horses cost the same to keep. If you plan to buy a horse for a specific job in a specific barn, then aside from insurance and unplanned vet bills, you essentially know your monthly budget for upkeep whether you pay $5,000, $50,000, or $500,000 for the horse.

I can already hear the horse people respond to my message above, saying, "You can't compare a $5,000 horse with a $500,000 horse." Sure, you likely wouldn't be talking about the same job for the horses at either end of that massive price range, but my point about ongoing cost comparison is valid. My fundamental message is this: Unless you're spending a shocking amount on a horse, **the biggest cost of**

buying a horse is almost always the ongoing upkeep, so buy the best horse you comfortably can, knowing that the few thousand dollars you have saved in the purchase price will be gone quickly in upkeep.

Pick a budget range that works for you and stick with it. One approach is to set the low end of the budget at what you're hoping to spend—and know you will be shown very few, if any, horses below the low end of your range once you set it. Set the high end of the budget at the top price you could go to, knowing that in order to do so you likely won't spend any money on showing for the next however many months to recover from going a bit overboard (and if you won't be showing anyway, then you may have a very narrow price range). Your trainer should be able to work within those boundaries; make sure they understand you will have to save money elsewhere to buy the higher-priced horse. And make sure to decline trying any horses outside your range.

Please also remember to consider the commission and other horse-shopping expenses in your price range. As an example, if you want to buy a horse in the $20,000 to $28,000 range, this is a breakdown of your actual out-of-pocket expenditures to get the horse into your care:

Note: These numbers are *illustrative*…fill in your own estimates!

	A "$20,000" horse	A "$28,000" horse
Travel to try horses	$700	$700
Pre-purchase exam (PPE)*	$2,000*	$2,000*
Purchase price	$20,000	$28,000
Ship horse to your barn	$800	$800
10 percent commission	$2,000	$2,800
Total purchase out of pocket	**$25,500**	**$34,300**

* Remember, you may do a PPE on one horse and decide to not buy that one, and then do one for the one you end up buying…that is, you may end up paying multiple PPE costs, so the numbers in this table are conservative. See further discussion of the pre-purchase exam starting on page 166.

Then consider some up-front costs that may show up early on:

	A "$20,000" horse	A "$28,000" horse
Insurance for the first year	$1,200	$1,500
New tack required	$500	$500
New blankets/fly masks	$400	$400
New halter with name plate*	$100	$100
Total additional out of pocket	**$2,200**	**$2,500**

---

*   I have found it physically impossible to buy a new horse and not buy him a fancy new halter with a name plate.

I hope for you that some of these line items are $0 when you do your math, but it's good to consider everything as these are real liabilities due immediately. And so, the total could be more like the following:

	A "$20,000" horse	A "$28,000" horse
Total purchase out of pocket	$25,500	$34,700
New tack required	$2,200	$2,500
Total additional out of pocket	**$27,700**	**$37,200**

Doing this math may change your thoughts on your price range, so just run a few back-of-the-napkin (or spreadsheet, if you like) scenarios to ensure you are fully prepared.

Like the full-ownership scenarios in the tables above, you apply the same logic to the costs of co-ownership or a full lease. Co-ownership costs are more obvious, but it is not uncommon for horses to lease out at 25 to 33 percent of their purchase price per year. When you lease, you can more easily progress through different horses that support your development. That is, you don't have to buy different horses at every stage, with all the risks discussed *ad nauseam* in this book. There are horses out there who may be able to perfectly develop with you for many years, but they can be hard to find.

Rideability and Chemistry

Even as a newcomer, you will have preferences. Some horses will feel more comfortable for you than others. This is linked to their experience (discussed below), but also their basic conformation and way of going. A horse with a huge athletic trot may be disconcerting for you in the early days, as you feel you're getting bounced out of the saddle. A horse that uses more of himself when going over any size jump or coming away from that first barrel may do the same. A horse built "uphill" with a comfortable "pocket" when you sit in the saddle may feel safer. There are many permutations. Listen to your trainer's perspective on the match, but tell them everything you love, like, and—when you are not around the horse at the time—anything you dislike about riding each horse you are trying. Your first impressions matter; trust your gut on this one. You should feel like you can work with and enjoy the horse when you start up the relationship.

Age, Experience, and Track Record

Unless you have taken years of lessons before you decide to lease or buy a horse, and likely even if you have, you first need to understand the horse world saying, "Green on green equals black and blue." The general point is when you are new ("green"), you should find a horse that is not also green—that is, one who knows his job far better than you. The risks are not just that you might fall off; they include potentially taking the horse backward, taking your riding backward— especially if you end up afraid of the horse's untrained behavior—and basically taking all the fun out of the journey of learning to ride and spending fulfilling time with horses.

Though age and experience do not always correlate exactly, they are directionally aligned. A five-year-old that has a future as a sport horse in any discipline needs years with someone qualified to bring him along. A ten-year-old with a good track record brings more experience with whatever discipline you intend to pursue. A fifteen-year-old likely has even more quality experience and can help you safely learn your craft. Of course, the exceptions to these patterns are a youngster who is as safe as they come, and an old guy who wasn't ever properly trained or perhaps was even mistreated and has terrible habits.

The obvious unfortunate factor with a very experienced horse is he is likely closer to retirement. Depending on the job you want him to do, his conformation, how well he has been cared for before you bought him, and how well you take care of him, it still is a bit of a wild card how long a horse will last for you as your sport partner. So, there is a constant balancing act when you are a newcomer in the horse world and want to buy a horse. I suggest you err on the side of experience for the horse and be prepared for the eventuality of his retirement. Retirement is not a bad thing; it simply changes your relationship with your horse. Indeed, my retired horses have always brought me great joy as I continue to care for them and spend time with them when possible (often they are in a different location where the prices for retirement farms are much lower).

Character, Size, and Color

Unless you are considering buying a horse you have previously leased, or he has been in your barn for a long time, it will be hard for you as a newcomer to judge his character. Observe everything you can about him from the second you arrive.

Your trainer will do the same. Evaluate his ground manners, whether he likes to be groomed, whether he is hunting treats—and possibly nipping for them, too—and so on. Also, ask everyone you meet at the trial barn what they think of the horse—whether he has bad habits, any funny stories, anything. Most people at the trial barn will be guarded in what they say, but pay attention and add the proverbial grain of salt to all of it.

The size of the horse matters, as you do not want one so large or so small that you look (and are) out of proportion when you are riding him. In part, you must ensure he can handle your weight and "take up your leg" (which is to say, your feet can't be seen far below the belly of the horse). The most challenging part of this is when you are buying a horse for your still-growing child rather than for your adult self. Discuss your child's growth expectations with the trainer and do your best from there (if your child is in a growth spurt or it is unclear how tall they will become, it may be safer to lease once or twice before buying).

Though many have favorites, the color and markings of a horse shouldn't really matter. My recommendation in this arena: Please don't let your affection for one particular horse color rule out a potential horse of the "wrong" color who just happens to be an amazing fit for you in terms of rideability, age, experience, character, size, and price.

Evaluation Approach (a.k.a., Horse Shopping!)

Horse shopping is at times exhausting (when you've tried several and nothing has come close) but is an incredible journey where you can learn a great deal about yourself, your riding, and your relationship with horses. You will likely get to meet and potentially ride several of these wonderful creatures. Be very conscious of every horse you meet in this process. Learn a bit about them (beyond the stats you no doubt already have before you show up) and mostly pay attention to everything when you meet them in person.

Evaluation Categories

The Horse Evaluation Template starting on page 178 includes the following categories of questions to evaluate:

- Price.
- Physical match.
- Riding match.
- Job match (includes expected longevity of fit for the job you want him to perform).
- Gut feel.
- Health and soundness (last in the list only because you engage your vet to finalize your thoughts in this topic, and thus it comes after everything else looks good).

Evaluation Steps

Like the Barn Evaluation Template, the Horse Evaluation Template may seem overly elaborate. My intention is to provide a comprehensive framework, and let you choose the bits that are important to you. I suggest you follow the following steps:

1. **Decide to buy.** Read this chapter in full and review the Horse Evaluation Template. Reflect on it, make sure you are serious enough to look, and think about your priorities. You do not need to commit to buying at this stage, but you should be serious when you start the process, so you are not wasting your time or that of everyone else involved. Talk with your partner or spouse, your kids (especially if the pony or horse is for one of them rather than you!), your friends, and generally whomever you usually talk to when you have to make an important life decision.

2. **Engage your trainer.** Bring up the idea with your trainer, presented as, "I'm considering buying a horse and would love your perspective on whether you think that is a good idea and what kind of horse might be good for me." Ask them to think about it for a bit, and then set up a time to talk about it (sure, they've probably already thought about it, but it is helpful to get this process going thoughtfully and slowly).

3. **Establish your criteria.** Have the sit-down with your trainer to discuss your priorities and their thoughts. Whether you use the Horse Evaluation Template or not—your trainer will likely scoff at something so ostensibly scientific in this very artistic process—you should be able to discuss the details of the following:

   » **Deal breakers:** These are the factors that are a "must have"—usually price range and a few others. If a horse does not meet this small set of criteria, then you should not waste anyone's time (especially your own brain time or heart time) thinking about him.

   » **Key requirements:** This is where you list your key criteria, the ones you will evaluate in total and make tradeoffs between, as it is a rare horse that will meet every criterion.

   » **Unicorn status:** Here is where you say you want a black mare with a star in the middle of her forehead who will let you cuddle with her when she is lying down in her stall, is totally broke and shows like a schoolmaster at only six years old, can take you from the puddle jumpers all the way to the big jumps, and will be able to do the job you plan for her until her early twenties! It is not a bad exercise to think about your unicorn, because the universe has a strange way of listening. The universe also has a strange way of finding you what you really need, and that young black mare could actually be a bay gelding in his early teens.

4. **Iterate with candidates.** This is the hard part. Your trainer and their horse professional colleagues all want to find you the right horse. Sure, the commission is an incentive, but they also love horses, and your making this step does make them happy and likely proud. You may cycle through these steps sequentially or have several candidates at once, but the basic flow is as follows:

» **Discuss:** Your trainer will bring up a potential horse with name, age, gender, show experience (if applicable), character, and (hopefully) why his owner is selling him. You review as many videos as are available, and then discuss the pros and cons and whether it is worth a trial.

» **Trial:** The trial allows you to meet and ride the horse under the supervision of your trainer, and most likely the horse's current trainer, unless the trainers know each other very well and have discussed in advance whether that is needed.

- See the section called "A Special Note on Trials" starting on page 165 for more details, but this is the vital step to determine whether you like the horse and indeed like riding the horse.

- One repeat thought from that section: If you do *not* like the horse for any reason, politely say so while giving huge thank-you pats to the horse, who has kindly had you on his back. If you have any negative critique, save it for when the horse has been returned to his stall or pasture.

» **Discuss (again):** After the glow of the trial wears off, you and your trainer will discuss the merits of the horse. In short, part of the goal is that you both believe you have a great chance at an amazing partnership with this horse in the coming years.

» **Negotiate:** Some horses are for sale at a firm number. Others come with some room to negotiate. The permutations are endless, but your trainer should be able to help you here. You figure out your highest number, they figure out their lowest, and if they are almost the same then you may have a deal.

» **Commit:** If the negotiation produces an agreement on price and any other terms, you then commit to the deal in a purchase and sale agreement, with the final sale pending the outcome of a pre-purchase examination and anything else you have agreed needs to be verified. Unless there is something significant that shows up in the pre-purchase exam, this is a done deal at this stage.

  - *Note that some people skip the purchase and sale agreement and go straight to a bill of sale. For reasons discussed in the section starting on page 173, that is not the optimal approach.* I once had an ostensibly fancy professional renege on a deal after this stage—even when the subsequent pre-purchase examination was clean. Their behavior was unprofessional at best, but because we hadn't signed a purchase and sale agreement, I was out of luck.

» **Pre-purchase examination:** The pre-purchase exam should be conducted by your trusted veterinarian, or another trusted veterinarian who does not currently treat the horse or have a professional relationship generally with the seller. See the section called "A Special Note on Pre-Purchase Examinations" starting on page 166 for full details, but this is the vital step in determining if this is still the horse for you.

» **Negotiate again, potentially:** It is possible that during the pre-purchase examination, the veterinarian finds something wrong with the horse. If it is a substantive issue, you may have a basis to renegotiate. If the seller disagrees and holds firm on the price, then you walk away and start the shopping process over. If the owner agrees, then you negotiate further and, potentially, lock in on a new price and set of terms.

Once you have found "the one," you are ready to execute the deal, per the section starting on page 167. But please don't skip the details on trials and pre-purchase examinations (starting on pages 165 and 166 respectively). You can't buy a horse without either of these vital steps.

Once you have found "the one," you are ready to execute the deal, per the section starting on page 167. But please don't skip the details on trials and pre-purchase examinations (starting on pages 165 and 166 respectively).

STORY

When You Least Expect It, They Find You

After many months of trying to figure out the best new job for my horse at the time, we had found him a fantastic home. Though a beautiful creature and brilliant mover, he turned out to be too spicy and spooky for me at that stage in my riding (or perhaps ever, if I'm honest). His lovely new mom was over the moon about him, and I was breathing a sigh of relief. I committed myself to a break from horse ownership, and the related expenses. And off I went from the dead of winter in Boston, without riding gear, to visit a friend in Wellington, Florida for a bit of sun and relaxation (and yes, horse watching).

Two days into my visit, my friend's trainer called to let her know that one of the horses in the barn needed to be sold quickly. The bay gelding in question was a 13-year-old 17.2-hand equitation horse; he was often leased out on weekends to whatever junior needed a solid ride for chasing points. If I had the cash available, I could become the proud new owner. When the trainer learned I was in town, he instructed to me to get some gear and head over to the barn for a trial.

And though I had just the night before pronounced my "I'm taking at least a six-month break from horse ownership" commitment, I figured, *Why not? What's the harm in at least trying him? And it seems like such a great deal!* I borrowed breeches and half-chaps from my friend, gloves and a helmet from the trainer's wife, bought new paddock boots, and off I went to meet and try this beautiful creature.

STORY CONTINUED

You know where this story is going. Of course I loved him. Of course I brought him home to Boston. The money from the sale of my prior horse was clearly burning a hole in my pocket, and my ideas about taking a break were delusional. I did get a pre-purchase exam done, so at least I wasn't completely reckless. I share this story because sometimes it can be okay to ignore some of the evaluation criteria in my fancy templates and simply honor it when the perfect horse finds you. Just stay aware of the risks; in this case, it was the combination of his age and previous level of hard work.

I had only three years of riding this horse before he needed to be retired; he had had a big career before me and had more than fulfilled anything the human world has a right to expect from a horse. In those three years, the stone wall he had built to protect himself during his career began to break down and his personality slowly and beautifully came out. He was perfection. He was one of my very small number of heart horses. And he enjoyed ten years of retirement in lovely Virginia, where he became even more expressive, before he passed away on his own one night—the night after I flew home to Florida after having visited him. I will forever believe, and be grateful, that he waited for me to kiss him one last time before crossing the rainbow bridge, and then—class act that he was—even saved me the difficult end-of-life decision process[*] by going on his own.[**]

---

[*]   For more on the topic of end-of-life care and decisions, please see the section starting on page 216.

[**]   It has been six years since this horse passed and as I write this—and as I read it repeatedly during the editing process—tears are streaming down my face. Someday maybe I can write about him or tell this story and not end up in tears, but I doubt it. And as a good friend who does energy work with horses said to me, sometimes we may not want to wish away tears that tell us so much.

A Special Note on Trials

When you meet a potential new horse on a trial, take a deep breath and tell him (silently, if you like) that he is beautiful, you are grateful for this time together, your intention is to be kind and ride as well as you can, you may screw up a bit when riding and you hope he will forgive you, and you wish him a beautiful future—whether or not you end up providing his forever home.

When you are riding in the trial, listen to your trainer (and perhaps the other trainer, if your trainer asks their opinion), be with the horse, sense what you are feeling, and remember as much as you can. If you have questions that need to be answered by trying something (for example, flying changes), then ask to do that so you have that information. When you are done, dismount, thank the horse once again, and then stand for just a few seconds—or a full minute if you can—and sense how you feel. Even though I have never been good at doing it, know that you are allowed to take a moment before you start talking (or listening to your trainer, for that matter). Use that moment to reflect: Are you excited about this horse? Do you think he liked you, or at least showed you a bit of himself in these early days? Do you feel like you rode better or worse than usual? What are your favorite things about the horse? What are your least favorite things?

Only once the horse has been taken back to the barn should you discuss the pros and cons of the horse. This often happens in trials because the discussion is rarely done in front of the other trainer. But—especially if there is something you really don't like about the horse—save it for later, when you are not on or near the horse. The horse you just rode may not be for you, but he is still an amazing creature, and likely putting up with lots of random people on his back lately (he may know what this process means, or at least be unsettled by the change to his normal life patterns). Please show him only kindness and love when you are in his perfect presence, and then politely move on in your horse-shopping journey.

A Special Note on Pre-Purchase Examinations

Completing a proper pre-purchase examination by a qualified objective veterinarian is table stakes for this process. It is heart-breaking when your dream horse—or even harder, your child's dream horse—has issues that are beyond what you want, or are able, to handle. You will get through it, I promise.

The question you are asking the veterinarian (hopefully one you know and trust, or at least one your trainer knows and trusts) is not, "Should I buy this horse?" The questions you are asking are:

- Given everything you know (based on bloodwork, complete X-rays, your physical exam on that day of the pre-purchase, available prior records if applicable, and so on), what do you think of this horse's prospects for the job I want him to do?
  - » Please note that there are different definitions of "complete" for X-rays and the litany of other tests and diagnostics one can do as part of a pre-purchase exam. Your trainer and your veterinarian are your counselors in this matter. If you go for the "full monty" in the exam, it will be expensive. If you try to save money and don't get X-rays of his feet, for example, it will likely be even more expensive in the long run.
- Do you believe there is any special maintenance this horse will need for a reasonably long life in that job?
- Are there any red flags that might impact a future sale if I later decide he is not the horse for me at some point in the future?

You should ask for a written report. I didn't know that was a thing for the first few horses I bought. In my early days, the veterinarian told my trainer, who then told me, for example, that the horse looked good and would likely stay sound with some periodic maintenance, and then I bought the horse. That is not the best model—again, my goal in this book is to share my missteps so you can avoid them. A veterinarian may have to add language in a written document that their lawyer tells them to (that nothing is certain in this world, this is their best professional opinion based on a view of this horse at a single point in time, and so on), but they should put in black and white what they observed, their professional opinion generally, and what makes them nervous (especially if they will be the one caring for the horse).

You should also feel free to ask your veterinarian what they didn't put on paper. I once had a vet tell me, effectively: "His X-rays are terrible for his age, but I've seen worse. So, though you won't be able to sell him with X-rays like that, with adequate maintenance you could have good fun with him for many years to come. You could also have a beautiful lawn ornament on your hands pretty soon, so be emotionally and financially ready for that." I so appreciated that thoughtful balanced counsel.

Close a Reasonable, Equitable, and Transparent Deal

Closing a reasonable, equitable, and transparent deal seems like a lofty objective in the horse world, but it is done every day. If you apply the same level of diligence as you would in the normal, "non-horse" world, you will be fine. Though horses pull at our heartstrings, it is not your job to save them all (though most of us want to). And though many horse people are not great businesspeople, it is not your job to support poor practices, let alone unethical ones.

And so, my recommendation is that you follow every rule you know about deal-making in the real world. Here are some of the basics I think apply, with a bit of a twist for their application in the horse world:

1. Protect yourself and those you love emotionally by remembering that a deal is never done until both the money and the horse have safely changed hands. Especially if you are buying a horse for your child, do all the work

appropriate for their age to manage their expectations and help them be less crushed if it doesn't work out for any number of reasons.*

2. Know your best-case scenario and true bottom line for the deal, and be prepared to walk away if the price or terms go outside your boundaries.

3. If you sense anyone is lying to you or trying to put one over on you, walk away (see below for ways to prevent and avoid this situation, but know it still happens).

4. If you're being told you must decide on the first day you see the horse or you'll "miss out," walk away.

5. Meet the other party in person if possible—unless they have abdicated their negotiation rights to a broker, in which case meet the broker—to understand their objectives and motivations (it is often not all about money) and share your own.

6. Do not negotiate with yourself. If you've made an offer, wait for the other party's response before responding; don't let your mind run amuck and think, "They're taking a while to respond, so I think I'll call them and improve my offer."

---

* One approach for managing expectations is simply not to tell your child until the deal is done. I once leased a horse to a young rider and the mother did just that. The fourteen-year-old girl missed the machinations of vet checks and negotiations (she had obviously tried the horse and loved him, but thought the idea was in the past). Then one day, she walked into the barn to find that big, beautiful gray waiting to nuzzle her. I may or may not have cried (okay, I did) when the mom sent me the video of those first moments after her daughter found out this was her new horse.

7. Do your homework on the horse and the people involved. There is plenty available on social media and public searches to know if the people involved, and the horse, are legitimate.

   » *Side note:* If you don't look up the horse's record in USEF.org or search for show videos, if applicable, when working on a deal to buy a horse, you are being almost as silly as if you had not had X-rays done of his feet as part of the pre-purchase exam (see the section starting on page 166 on that topic).

8. My final couple of bits:

   » If you are buying a horse…do not buy halters with nameplates or any other personalized gear until the deal is complete. This is more a superstition of mine than concern about the money you could waste on such things…in short, don't jinx the deal. I also think it's polite to pay your trainer's commission before buying special gear for the new horse.

   » If you are selling a horse…do not spend the money before the deal is complete, and don't forget you (likely) must still pay that commission to (at least) your trainer.

Price: Avoid Hidden Costs

When buying a horse, you need to be very clear about your budget and stick with it. You then need to look only in that price range. And then…you need to make sure that you aren't being told a price that you can afford, but that the horse isn't worth. And that last bit is the hard part. The section starting on page 60 introduces this concept, and the section starting on page 254 talks further about the ongoing dilemma of being a target if you have what is viewed as "plenty" of money. Though this is a bit of a restatement of those other sections, here are some things I suggest:

- **Talk directly with the other party.** In a case where the seller has no idea some middle people are adding cost, this will help. If the seller is in on it—as in, they are keeping some or all of the extra—this tactic may not help much.
- **Exchange money directly with the other party.** Again, this helps with the unwitting seller only.
- **Query the professionals you trust.** If you have any concerns about pricing or commissions, sit down in a serious way with your trainer or broker (not when passing each other in the barn aisle) and ask your questions. If they lie to you in that conversation and you find that out later, then—at a minimum—you leave them.
- **Talk with friends and scour social media.** It can always be helpful to talk with friends (horsey ones or not) about purchases. Indeed, the section starting on page 109 describes how you might use a horse budget accountability partner. And though a long shot, sometimes a rigorous search of social media can produce interesting results.

There are times when things are too complex for you to be certain you are not being charged a bit extra, and so then you must decide whether you want the horse even when you believe someone is making some extra money off you somewhere. I did this once. I knew there had to be one more player in the mix getting a slice I was funding, but I decided in that unique scenario I was okay with it.

Terms: Avoid Undue Exposure and Risk

This section goes along with the section starting on page 97 related to securing the right legal counsel. You need to think through all the things that matter to you and list them out. Relevant terms include:

- Timing of the transaction (dates for money, horse transfer, and so on).
- Methods of payment required (so you can have your money in the right place).
- Term (when it is for a lease).
- Responsibility for shipping the horse.
- Timing of transfer of risk, and thus responsibility for insurance (for example, who has responsibility when, in relation to the transaction dates).
- Right of first refusal on resale (this is an optional term that may be considered).

There are also many legal terms related to assumption of risk, governing law, forum choice, and more; those are typically less contentious.

Documentation: Put Everything on Paper for Everyone Involved to See

As discussed in the section discussing "Legal Considerations" starting on page 97, when it comes to a substantive deal for a lease or purchase, you should have everything written down. With a formal contract (purchase and sale agreement, bill of sale, lease agreement, lease agreement with option, or consignment agreement, to list a few), you should include an "entire agreement" clause to reflect that the entire agreement is solely what is on the that document, and does not include anything that might have been brought up in conversations or emails, or on other bits of paper. With the right counsel, this will be easy, but even with counsel you should read everything in detail yourself and make sure you are comfortable.

I also recommend making sure the key people involved all get a copy of the same final, executed (fully signed) document. For the trainers and brokers, if applicable, this should be the basis for their commissions. The document should also clarify that the seller and buyer are responsible independently for any commissions they owe.

Commissions: Avoid Hidden Commissions

Almost without exception, you will pay your trainer a commission to help you buy or sell a horse. When buying a horse, your trainer will review potential options with their circles of professional friends, sale barns, brokers, social media, and sometimes traditional media (for example, horse magazines). They will get all the basic details and watch any videos provided by the seller. They will work with you on any of the options worth a trial and go with you on those trials. They often handle the negotiations and all the details related to the sale. They also provide their professional opinion about whether each horse could be a good match for you. You should know from your barn search, but you can also ask at the barn if your trainer has a good reputation for finding quality horse matches. Some are exceptional, others adequate, and a few are terrible.

The commission for their services is typically 10, 15, even 20 percent. You will pay that amount if you buy the first horse you try. You will pay that amount if you buy the tenth horse you try. The former scenario can be frustrating, just like with a real estate broker who makes the same commission regardless. Unlike the shifts in real estate commission structures today, the horse world is pretty set with this one-size-fits-all model. If you want to negotiate a different deal, do it upfront. Do not wait until after you buy the first horse you tried and then complain about having to write such a big check for what seemed like very little work. Remember that it may seem like very little work to you, but the outcome is more likely based on their years of experience and deep connections—that's why they were able to find you a good option quickly. **You are not paying them for their hours, you are paying them for their years.**

When discussing the commission structure and amount, make sure you clarify with your trainer that you are agreeing to pay their commission and no others. Document your agreement with your trainer in this regard. If any other professional involved in the transaction expects some payment, that is up to your trainer and not you, unless you agree to it in advance. Though the seller is typically responsible for their trainer's and, if applicable, the broker's commission, there are often professionals in the middle who make connections. These connections are valuable because they help your trainer find you a horse, but it should not be another commission for you to pay. See the section starting on page 62 regarding how to close the deal so additional commissions are less likely to be hidden in what you pay.

Steps to Close the Deal and Transition the Horse

After a couple (or several) iterations of the "evaluation steps" above, you will hopefully have an agreed-upon deal. To close the deal as the buyer, you need to execute the following critical steps. Anytime you transition a horse (even when it is already your horse and you are just moving barns), you need to be just as thoughtful about item 4, Horse Transition Document, and item 7, Horse Transition, as you do during the purchase process.

1. **Purchase and sale agreement (P&SA):** Many people will skip this step and put all deal terms into a *bill of sale*. But just as you would with a house, you want to commit in writing to the terms of the deal before conducting the pre-purchase exam and any other steps required to close the deal. The P&SA will include many standard warranties and warranty disclaimers, but all of it should be reviewed by a qualified attorney if possible. Only upon signatures from both buyer or buyer's agent and seller or seller's agent do you have an executed deal.

2. **Pre-purchase exam:** Upon having a signed P&SA, you can conduct the pre-purchase exam. What you learn from the pre-purchase exam may impact your willingness as the buyer to move forward or it may change your view of the price you are willing to pay.

3. **Insure the horse:** If you are the buyer and plan to insure the horse, get a "rider" from your insurance agency before you sign any documents or transfer money. The exact point when legal ownership shifts from seller to

buyer should be made clear in the P&SA; if it is not, this can be a source of legal battles later if something happens to the horse during the transition.

4. **Horse transition document:** The seller should prepare for you—as early as possible, given that you will likely need to buy or arrange things before the horse arrives—all the details they believe are relevant to ensuring the horse has a smooth transition into your care. This includes some of the obvious things (for example, date of last shoeing, vaccination status, feed, supplements, and so on) and hopefully some of the nuances, too (specifics on tack and bits, how he does in turnout, whether he needs earplugs when riding). You will find a Horse Transition Template in the section starting on page 181.

5. **Money transfer to owner:** The only interesting thing about this step is that sometimes there is a broker involved who receives your money and then passes along the funds to the owner.

6. **Bill of sale:** The seller should send you a draft of the bill of sale to review, typically when they send you the draft purchase and sale agreement. If you have a complex deal that was fully documented in a purchase and sale agreement, your bill of sale can be quite simple (and thus easy to share as needed with any associations). Upon receipt of the money, they should then send the signed bill of sale for you to sign as well and return.

7. **Horse transition:** As the buyer, you will typically arrange and pay for shipping the horse to your barn. Whether you or your trainer make the arrangements, make sure everyone involved is clear on a good date for the horse to ship (for example, a date such that he hasn't been in recent heavy stress, just vaccinated, just shod, and so on). You should also try to have your horse arrive early enough in the day that you and others will be

around for many hours. Especially if it has been a long journey, you want to make sure your horse is settled, eating, drinking, peeing, and—importantly—pooping long before people go home for the night.[*]

8. **Money transfer to trainer:** Though it is painful after spending all that money for the horse, vetting, shipping, and more, you likely have a commission to pay as well. Unless you have arranged something different with your trainer, they are reasonable to expect you to pay it promptly.

9. **Change owner of record with USEF and other associations:** The previous owner can complete this step for any associations where the horse is registered. As the buyer, you can also complete this step with a bill of sale signed by the previous owner. If the broker signs the bill of sale rather than the previous owner, you will need the previous owner to complete a simple "transfer of ownership" document. The USEF website is pretty good for completing this step online.

What to Do When You Have the Wrong Horse for You

This is one of the hardest challenges of horse ownership. Sometimes, even though you love a horse deeply, you must face the reality that the two of you are not a good match. The reasons for this can be many. One simple scenario is that the horse is physically not up to the higher level of riding you want to move up to (in whatever discipline); it is best to make the decision early rather than pushing him beyond his natural abilities and risking his near- and long-term soundness.

---

[*] When you are a proud member of the horse world, you will have many pictures of manure on your phone. Sometimes, as here, it is to celebrate your new arrival demonstrating to you that his system appears to be working fine. Most of the rest of the manure photos will be when you are monitoring whether his overly-loose or overly-dry manure has improved in consistency. Your barn and vet will instruct you on such things.

Remember from the section on page 19 that a horse has this right: "To be in a job that suits his body, character, age, and natural abilities (know that sometimes this implies he might be best suited to be a magnificent lawn ornament)."

Be Honest With Yourself: Sometimes It's Not a Good Match

Sometimes, the situation is more complex. It may be a combination of factors; you might find it feels unsafe, frustrating, too hard, scary, unpredictable, or simply no longer fun riding your horse. This may be obvious soon after you have leased or bought the horse, but it may show up months or years later. An early first regression can be a normal part of the journey; you will get through it, so don't give up right away. However, if you and your trainer have tried everything and you are not able to get your mojo back with this horse—the mojo you had during the trial, or perhaps in your early days together—over many months or even years, you may need to consider selling the horse.

For much of my horse career, the idea of selling a horse seemed terrible. Surely nobody else would love and take as good care of this horse as me, right? What I have learned is that there is a great match for every person and every horse. If you regularly have any of the feelings above (fear, uncertainty, unhappiness), your horse feels that too and it will be no more fun for him than it is for you. If you sell the horse in a compassionate way—work hard to find him the best forever home, and perhaps include a right of first refusal so they can't sell him on to someone terrible—you most often are doing him a favor. You need to do right by the animal, and you also need to do right by yourself, and so you may have to find both of you a better match.

Be Honest With the Horse World: Sometimes It's the Horse

If the words "unsafe" or "scary" above ring true at any point in your horsey career, sometimes it means you are just not up to handling that particular horse's level of what I call "spicy," and that is completely reasonable. Others will say "hot," or "blood," or any number of terms. Horses with those adjectives are not for me—I will love on them until the end of time without riding them—and yet they are absolutely horses for other horse people.

And here is the big "but"…but you must share the full story about the horse when you decide he is not for you. When I sold my "spicy" horse, I had told them every bad thing that beautiful creature had done—that I knew about. They weren't bothered (braver than me, clearly) and it was a great match. In that scenario, the buyer was an experienced adult. But imagine if the buyer had been a newcomer, or—arguably worse—a newcomer who was also a child. Imagine someone wants to offload their seemingly sweet (yet spicy) horse, isn't forthcoming about periodic really bad behaviors, and knows the newcomer's trainer isn't very experienced and just wants to get a deal done. Then remember this is a dangerous sport and people get hurt, and you will understand the potential for a spiral into the land of litigation.

Please give people and horses the best chance of success by being as transparent as possible when you need to find your horse a new home. It is hard to swallow when you have a horse who isn't what you thought he would be when you bought him—trust me, I have spent many tears, hours, and dollars in this way. But kicking the can down the road to someone else is neither ethical nor, in my opinion, humane (to either humans or horses).

Templates
Horse Evaluation Template

Horse Barn Name	
Registered Name	
Short Description (age, height, breed, gender, color, markings)	
Owner	
Date of Trials	
Horse USEF #	
Trainer	
Vet (if known)	
Farrier (if known)	

Category	Questions	Notes
Price	1. Why is the current owner selling or leasing the horse? 2. What is the asking price or lease fee? Did the owner or intermediary indicate any flexibility on those numbers? 3. Are there other things of value to the owner in the deal (for example, a good home, staying in the area, a certain job, a certain barn for a lease)? 4. Are there other things the owner might be willing to offer (for example, a lease-with-option-to-buy)? 5. For a lease, are you clear on all the cost responsibilities (see pages 147-50)?	

HORSE EVALUATION TEMPLATE CONTINUED

Category	Questions	Notes
Physical Match	**6.** Is the horse's temperament and personality aligned with what you like so far in horses (more in gut feel)? **7.** Does he have any bad behaviors or vices (that you have seen or the owner shared)? **8.** Is he a good size for you or your child? And do you feel comfortable (that is, at ease and safe) with him? **9.** If your child is still growing, does everyone's best bet say he will still be a good size match in the coming years?	
Riding Match	**10.** If you think the horse could be a contender, were you able to try him *at least twice?* **11.** How does his natural "motor" feel to you? That is, do you have to work hard to get him to go, about in the middle, or you work more to keep him from going fast? Do you have a preference? **12.** How does his stride feel to you at the walk, trot, and canter? Even though he is new to you, you can assess whether you feel a preference for his natural movement: Is the walk slow or fast? Is the trot smooth or more athletic and bouncy? Is the canter easy to sit or a little harder for you?	
Job Match	**13.** Does this horse have experience with new-comers, and is he known to be forgiving with the mistakes we all make at an early stage of riding? **14.** Given you are a newcomer, how often should this horse have a professional ride to stay in top physical and behavioral form? **15.** How much experience does this horse have with exactly the job you want him to do? **16.** If you want to compete, does his track record bode well for your objectives?	

Category	Questions	Notes
Job Match	**17.** Do you have other aspirations for his job (for example, do you want to move up to a different level)? If so, how much experience does he have at that level? **18.** If he hasn't done the level you aspire to someday, does your trainer have experience developing horses to advance in that manner?	
Gut Feel	**19.** Do you think he is beautiful, and did you want to kiss his nose when you met him? **20.** Was his presence and energy at ease and felt good to you when you connected with him in turnout, his stall, cross-ties, ring, trail, and so on (as much as you had the chance to experience)?	
Health and Soundness	**21.** Did the owner share any details regarding any supplements, medication, or maintenance to stay healthy and sound? **22.** How hard has he worked in his life, and might that impact his longevity? **23.** If the horse is currently living in a different geography/climate, does everyone believe he can adapt to your location? **24.** Were you (and your vet) able to see his prior veterinary records? **25.** What were the results of the Pre-Purchase Exam, and what does that imply for his suitability to the job you want him to do and any support he will need to stay sound and fit in that job for years to come (see pages 166-67)?	

Horse Transition Template

Barn Name	
Registered Name	
Owner	Name, phone #
Prior Vet	Name, phone #
Date	
Horse USEF #	
Prior Trainer	Name, phone #
Prior Farrier	Name, phone #

	Last Date	Typical frequency	Handles well? Any typical reactions?
Care			
Shoeing			
Dental			
Chiropractor			
Other:			
Other:			
Medical			
Fecal Egg Count			
Worming			
Ulcer/Gastro-Guard			
Other:			
Other:			

	Last Date	Typical frequency	Handles well? Any typical reactions?
Vaccinations			
Flu/Rhino			
Rabies			
EEE/WEE			
Tetanus			
West Nile			
Botulism			
Other:			
Other:			

Horse reaction to:	Handles well? Any typical reactions? Any special care needed?
Turnout	
Treadmill/hotwalker	
Trail rides	
Shipping	
Showing	

Typical Feed Schedule	Morning	Mid-Day (if applicable)	Evening	Night Check
Approximate Time				
Feed				
1.				
2.				
3.				
4.				
Supplements/ medications				
1.				
2.				
3.				
3.				
3.				
Hay				
1.				
2.				

Horse Gear	Any recommendations welcome!
Bridle and bit	
Saddle and girth	
Other tack	
Ear plugs and/or bonnet	
Blankets (including sizing)	

Chapter Six

Build the Right Care Team—One Ready to Support Your Equine Athlete

When You Own a Horse, Building His Care Team Is Your Primary Job

Building and managing the best possible horse care team you can find is job one. As a newcomer, when you are not equipped to do much of anything yourself, you must use your brain power and people skills to do what is right for your horse. Everything in this section is designed to help you ask the right questions and fulfill your role as an advocate, protector, and champion for your equine athlete.

Throughout this book, I use the term "horse care team" to mean everyone engaged in one or more elements of your horse's care. The structure presented in this chapter essentially mirrors the structures in Chapter 3 starting on page 47. Yet there are a few additions, as there will be some members of your team who don't cost you money (read: friends and family who might only cost you the price of their meal if you want a really long conversation about your horse).

The table below is organized by the "who" (describing the various roles) and then the "what" (as in what those people or teams do to help your horse and you). When you start with horses, you will most likely engage the providers your trainer and barn have as their "primary." Over time, you should feel free to engage new professionals. This brings us to the idea of a "closed barn."

A "closed barn" typically means you must use all the care professionals specified by the barn. In any barn, but especially the large ones, this is primarily to help the whole barn system run smoothly. In a "closed barn," you would not be allowed to have a different vet or farrier. In a more flexible barn, you could engage somebody else, but you would likely be expected to manage everything personally, as the barn system won't function well with everyone having their own choice of every care team member. Every barn should be flexible on bringing in specialists as needed. There are barns that have a "closed barn" model because they have either a personal or financial relationship with the providers. There is nothing wrong with that if it doesn't cost you anything and you trust the providers, but you have a right to understand the circumstances.

Understand the Key Roles in Your Team

The "Who"	The "What"
Trainer(s)	Your trainer is like the general contractor of your horse project. In the early days of horse ownership, they will not only manage the rest of the horse care team, but they will also make the recommendations you will (somewhat blindly) follow. The quality of your trainer could be judged by these simple principles: • A good trainer puts your horse's and your interests first. • A great trainer educates you every step of the way, so you can add more value in your owner role. • A poor trainer says, "Trust me," and limits your learning so you stay bewildered by it all and beholden to them. I have had all the above. I've learned that truly poor trainers are not fixable; walk away. I have also learned that most "good" trainers are only not "great" because most horse owners do not show enough consistent interest to be worth their efforts to educate them. So…getting from good to great is candidly up to you, not them. Ask questions, take it seriously, and be consistent about it.

The "Who"	The "What"
Barn manager and staff	The barn manager and staff run the system that cares for your horse. They ensure the right feeding, care, vaccinations, and so on. The more professional the barn, the more visible this all will be to you. The more you try to learn what is happening, the better you will grow to be as a horse parent.
Grooms	Never, ever doubt who in the full horse care team knows your horse best. It is the groom team. They spend the most time with and around your horse. They know your horse's quirks and patterns, and thus they are often the first to notice if something doesn't seem right. Get to know your grooms and thank them for all that they do in whatever ways you are able.
Farrier	No feet, no horse. The farrier is massively important. Bad shoeing can lead to many problems. Great shoeing can both keep a horse sound and remedy body problems that come from the feet. Most barns have a farrier that they use, and they expect you to use them too. If you want to use someone else and it's a large barn, you will need to manage the process (make sure their planned visit times are okay and be there with them).
Veterinarians	Equine vets are incredible humans who deal with every stage of a horse's life. They are there for the scary times, and they are often the only ones there at end of life to help them over the rainbow bridge (few owners will be there for that, though often a trainer or barn staff will be). There are several types of vets, and every one of them is valuable.
Primary equine vet	Your PEV is just like your PCP (primary care physician). They are your all-around vet, though they may also specialize. They keep track of all the basics…blood work, vaccinations, fitness, most wounds or soundness issues, and more. If you are a very lucky horse owner, you won't need anyone else.
Soundness vet	The soundness vet does not have a special degree *per se*, they have simply developed a specialization in being able to see what is making a horse off and fixing it. Quite often, this is your PEV. Or it may be someone else. Just make sure you know the roles and who can add the most value depending on the problem your horse is presenting.

The "Who"	The "What"
Specialists and surgeon vet	There are as many specialists in the horse health world as in the human health world. There are ophthalmologists for horses, and there are surgeons who specialize in equine dental surgery. When you need a specialist, your PEV or SV will recommend one. When the situation is complicated, ask for a second opinion.
Dentist	Horses need their teeth "floated" regularly. This is a process that removes sharp edges—which show up as horses' teeth continue to grow and wear down over time—from the teeth to improve chewing, and should be done by a quality equine dentist every 6–12 months. The dentist will also keep an eye on any suspect teeth, as infection is always possible, and that might merit removal.
Chiropractor	Equine chiropractors can be magic. They can tell where pain is coming from and adjust your horse to be comfortable in his body. Many people see this care as optional, as they do for their own bodies, but I have found it more than helpful even when used just periodically.
Acupuncture	Like chiropractic work, acupuncture can be very helpful for some horses and certain conditions. Every one of these modalities must be measured against the value you feel your horse gets for the money spent. Do everything in this table and you have an expensive care routine. Use each professional's services selectively when needed, and you will help your horse both feel more comfortable and stay sounder longer.
Bodywork and massage	A good body worker can do wonders for your horse's balance, comfort, and even attitude. This is about real bodywork, not just a nice rub down (that's called a curry-comb grooming, and you or your groom team should be doing that for your horse regularly already). This is also about getting expert feedback about how your horse is doing, where he might be stuck in his body, and anything you can do to help him be more comfortable.
Private parts cleaning	This part of your horse's care team is important, for both boy and girl horses. Yes, girls need this too. It is also something people tend not to like to do, so it can be "forgotten"; do your horse a favor and make sure this is done regularly (at least a couple times a year, if not more, depending on your horse's body, environment, and job). There are experts in this area of horse care…if you can find one, I highly recommend it; they not only do a more thorough job, but they are better equipped to notice anything unusual.

The "Who"	The "What"
Insurance provider	The section starting on page 106 talks about the options for, and pros and cons of, insurance. At a minimum, consider major medical insurance. You may pay the premiums for years without having to use it (as I have), but when it is finally needed (as I finally did with a unique dental surgical problem), it makes the decision process for your horse's treatment less stressful.
Barn and horsey friends	When it comes to the care of your horse, there are lots of opinions. You will learn who to trust over time, but generally the horse world works on a "I had a horse with XYZ once that is similar" basis. So please take it all with a grain of salt and check any ideas with your medical professionals. Sometimes genius ideas come this way, truly, but it can take sifting through random irrelevant ideas to get there.
The internet	If you have the time to do a proper job in your online research, you can find helpful information on the internet in the right forums. And by "a proper job," I mean finding relevant articles, verifying key points using multiple sources, and hopefully finding some relevant research from a reputable source that backs up any claims you come across. Posting a question on a horsey site or blog and listening to what the first few people who happen to respond say does not count as proper research. And save your equine medical professionals' time by not asking them about such randomly sourced ideas (unless subsequent research indicates it might be valid). I have found it more than helpful even when used just periodically.
Friends and family	The non-horsey people in your life can add value. Primarily, they can listen to you talk things through and show empathy for your situation as you grapple with health care decisions for your horse. They can also ask good questions that might be based on their human or other animal care experience, and sometimes spark a helpful idea. Leverage your friends and family on this journey. Just keep the number of hours on the topic to a level where they won't hide from you when the next horse health drama pops up.
Your own fitness and medical team	You can do a great job with everything above relating to your horse, and still struggle if you are weak, stuck in your body, off-balance, unhappy, inflexible, and so on. One of my favorite chiropractors told me she knows the one thing that is wrong with every horse, and that is his rider. This doesn't make us bad people; it just means we need to understand that if we don't show up happy, healthy, fit, and balanced, we will not be engaging with our horses in the most constructive way possible.

Establish a Clear Engagement Model with Your Horse Care Team

Model A—Your Trainer and Barn Handle Most Everything for You

Whether you are simply too busy to be on point for most of the care your horse needs, or you feel you don't know enough to take on the responsibility, having your trainer and the team at your barn handle most everything is a perfectly fine, and indeed normal, model. You are still ultimately responsible and accountable; you are just leaning heavily on the horse care team you have built. You show up to ride, make decisions when asked or decide to insert yourself, and the rest is done for you.

When I was working 24/7 and traveling the world, this was my model. And yet, I could have done it much better. I failed many times at being the best advocate for my horse due to both ignorance and lack of attention. The section starting on page 218 includes a template for a Horse Care Plan to help you avoid the mistakes I made in my early years of horse ownership. Sit down with your trainer and barn manager to go over it. Get their feedback so you can edit it to fit your circumstances and their business. This exercise helps both horses and humans stay healthy and happy. If your barn balks at such a dialogue, consider if you want to work with people who aren't willing to talk about expectations, roles, and responsibilities.

The section starting on page 221 includes a template for a Horse Care Tracker to help you keep track of all major health care interventions in each year. One of my trainers did a version of this for every horse in her barn. I borrowed the structure and have evolved it over the years for my own horses. This tool forces me to keep track of my horse's care (beyond searching through my email for various bills) and helps me communicate accurately and completely with all members of my care team. I keep mine in a plastic sheet protector (along with Coggins, Horse Care Plan, Insurance Notification Instructions, Emergency Care Authorization, and so on) in my trunk. It is always there for anyone who needs to know.

Model B—You Track and Manage All of the Interventions Yourself

When you are brand new to horses, this model can be difficult and potentially dangerous. However, if you have someone to supervise you and keep eyes on your horse, do as much of the work as you have time to take on. Having experienced eyes on your horse is critical. Do not let these massive powerful creatures fool you. They are incredibly delicate. Not noticing a stocked-up (swollen) leg early enough can turn a small problem into something big. Not realizing your horse is a bit lame can do more damage to him, and potentially to you if he is in enough pain to want you off his back. Not seeing and understanding the signs of colic early enough could lead, bluntly, to death.

You are not doing a good job at being a protector for your horse if you go it alone too early. You should of course feel free to do as much of the stall mucking, water lugging, and horse grooming as you like. Just have someone check your work. Trust me, mucking stalls is not as easy as it might appear. Use the Horse Care Plan on page 218 to see what you think you can do and where you need help. Use the Horse Care Tracker on page 223 to keep track of everything in one place.

Model C—You Agree on a Hybrid Model That Works for You All

If you do the Horse Care Plan well, you can create a working model. Do know that most barns only offer a couple board options—otherwise pricing and billing would be too complicated (see the section starting on page 86 for the detailed models). Because of that, you will likely need to pay for whatever set plans are available. However, if you are consistent and go with the flow of the barn, you can always take on certain tasks that would otherwise be done by the barn. When I'm in a full care situation (where my horse will be groomed and tacked up for me), I like to do my own grooming, tacking up, untacking, bath, and so on when I have time. I just need to let people know when that will be the case, and then follow through so I don't confuse everyone.

Learn the Fine Art of Challenging, and Sometimes Changing, Your Team

Though we all hope to find the right trainer, vet, farrier, and more the first time out and keep them forever, it rarely works that way. You might go months or many years with the same team, but for various reasons you will need to change team members at some point along the way. This section is designed to help you navigate these situations. Though much of it comes down to the personalities involved, and you will know them best, that didn't stop me from creating a framework to help you think things through.

Understand the Range of Drama You May Create with Challenges and Changes

Some members of your care team will respond to being queried, challenged, or changed more professionally than others; those who have been doing this for a long time and are confident in their skills, what they offer, and themselves are generally easier to deal with.

I think of these challenges and changes as creating a range of complexity to manage given a corresponding range of emotion level; each level of emotion generates a typical response from the impacted team members.

- **Green: "That's a pity, but it makes sense and I totally understand."** These come from life events (for example, you move to a new area, or you need specialist skills for a unique health situation with your horse). Generally, nobody's feelings are hurt; if anyone escalates something in this category into "barn drama," consider walking away in full.

- **Yellow: "I'm disappointed and don't think you need to change or adjust anything, but I understand and we're good."** These result from personal preferences (for example, you choose a specialist outside the practice of your primary vet because they have deeper skills, or you want a second opinion from someone new). Some people may be a bit bothered, as they would have preferred another choice, but they're not offended—or at least won't publicly say they are offended, as there is no reasonable basis to be so.

- **Red: "What are you thinking? Who have you been talking to about this? Don't you trust me/us? Have you been going behind our backs?"** These changes are typically sourced from substantive issues that have occurred or a strong difference of opinion (for example, you want to get a second opinion for a routine treatment the barn vet does for all the other horses in the barn). This is when you will get a sense of the level of professionalism of the member(s) of the care team you're questioning. It will also give you a sense of whether horse welfare, or your welfare, or the professional's feelings and reputation come first.*

Do Your Own Thinking on the Topic before Challenging or Changing

Even as an absolute newcomer, there will be times when something doesn't feel right to you. It could be something obvious (for example, you found your horse's water bucket empty…yes, you have a right to point this out and ask how the care team will ensure it doesn't happen again) or something more nuanced (your horse appears to be rubbing his tail a bit more when in his stall…yes, it's worth finding out if this is a new thing or perhaps you just haven't noticed before). You should trust your gut and ask the question—but do it nicely, as it could be your error.

---

* As you can tell throughout this book, my strong perspective is that horse welfare should trump all other priorities (other than human physical safety, of course). You should not retain a vet you believe is not good for your horse, even if it incenses any humans involved. I am not implying you will always be right, and you need to think through such things and indeed make sure you have a better option before upsetting the apple cart, but you should try not to have care team members' feelings as a criterion for your decision.

Many times I have said, "Wow, that's new," only to have folks in the barn say, "Actually, it's been that way for a while." Before you get offended at being told you missed something, know that when you are new, there are so many details it is easy for not all of them to make it into the long-term memory bank. Just the other day, I noticed a horse in my barn that I've known for over a year (granted, from afar, as I've never groomed or ridden him) had black polka dots on his front white socks. His Dalmatian-looking ankles are darn cute, but not new. I just never noticed them.

After an initial query on any topic bothering you, do some research to see what you can find. This mostly comes into play if a veterinarian or other medical professional gives you a prognosis and a recommended treatment plan. Even if you think you agree with the plan, dig in to learn more about it. If you hear the word "ulcer," start researching "horse ulcers" and see what you can learn. You should not endeavor to play the role of Dangerous-Dr-Google, but if you do some basic research, you will be able to ask more informed questions. You will also better comprehend the answers from your care professional, as the related lingo will already be familiar.

Get an Insider Perspective

Once you have given it serious thought and done research on your own, you should tap into your horsey friends and other members of the care team. I put this after doing your independent work as it is very easy to be swayed by the first person you talk to if you haven't dug into the topic already. If you ask about ulcer treatments, one friend may say, "You'll be fine if you go with the plan they're suggesting," and a care team member might say the same. But if you've already done your research, you can ask about the source of their opinion, efficacy of treatment options, length of treatment, issues with the treatment over time, yada yada.

Sometimes a bit of research and talking to a few people will make you comfortable with the recommended path forward. Other times, it will be either really confusing, or a high-cost or high-risk path, such that you're still uncomfortable. When that happens, move along to the next step.

Get a Formal Second Opinion

As with human medical care, there are certain procedures or treatment protocols where a second opinion is almost always appropriate (as long as it is not time critical). In cases when second opinions are normal, it is typically a veterinarian giving the advice and they should totally understand your desire to get a second opinion. Indeed, they will often recommend it themselves.

It can get more complicated when you are questioning something most people are saying is normal or routine. For example, if your horse has had multiple treatments (for example, hock injections) from the same vet, and you are starting to believe the treatments are too frequent, but the vet tells you it's normal and not to worry about it, it is a somewhat delicate matter to bring in a new soundness veterinarian. However, it is worth discussing, as there are many opinions on frequency and type of treatment, and the range of options is wide. Importantly, you may also be treating a secondary symptom rather than the root cause.

Nothing in this book counts as medical advice, but the reason for the Horse Care Tracker on page 221 is to help you monitor trends. Issues happen and treatments are needed, but noticeable shifts in frequency are important to monitor.

My final message, in summary:

- *Trust your gut.*
- If you're not convinced of the advice you are being given and/or there are potential or real costs in terms of horse health, ***get a second opinion***.

Decide to Change a Team Member

There will be times in the evolution of your horse journey when you will need to make a change to a horse care team member. Sometimes it is simply that your needs have changed, and you believe you can find another place more prepared to help you in the next stage. This is often the case if you shift barns or trainers while staying in the same geographical area. You love your trainer, but you feel there is another situation better suited to you. You might even really love your trainer, but your aging horse simply needs larger paddocks, and they don't have that available at your current barn. The reasons for no-drama shifts are many, but it's still a hard decision to make.

There are also times when you have a concern, and your attempts to remedy it with the relevant team member have not worked. In these cases, you shouldn't be surprised if the team member is hurt, angry, offended, or whatever is their go-to negative emotion. You are essentially telling them that you no longer fully trust them in one way or another. For example, it could be that you no longer trust them to:

- Be honest with you and operate with transparency.
- Charge you a reasonable amount for their goods and/or services.
- Respond in a reasonable timeframe.
- Show up on time and give you sufficient time.
- Care sufficiently about your horse's and your interests.
- Not talk about your horse or you behind your back.
- Exhibit good judgment in horse care and/or rider training.
- Demonstrate good competence in horse care and/or rider training.
- Do the right thing for you—generally, and even if they will make less money doing said right thing.
- Do a good job—generally, or in a way that preserves your horse's or your health and safety.

- Treat your money and financial situation with respect.
- Treat your horse with respect, or not endanger them in any way.
- Treat you, and your child, with respect.

Making a change doesn't always mean you don't trust their judgment or competence, but it will still likely be an ego hit for them. Aside from very few exceptions, most people will take being "fired" as an affront to their abilities, integrity, or whatever is their go-to negative assumption.*

One fundamental part of deciding to change a team member is finding what you believe to be a better alternative. If you are hunting for a new barn, it is a very delicate process to start asking around to see what might be better for you (see Chapter 4 starting on page 47 for more on the topic of evaluating potential barns and trainers). If you want a different chiropractor, it is much less delicate, and yet you must find someone that is willing to come to your barn. And if you want to replace a barn-standard team member (the primary vet who does all vaccinations and worming, or the farrier who shoes all the horses), you need to see whether your barn is going to manage a new person coming in or require that you be there in person yourself.

Transition a Team Member

Once you make the decision to change a team member, you need to execute the transition professionally. The section starting on page 181 provides a Horse Transition Template; use that, along with instructions number 4 and 7 on page 174, anytime you change your horse's barn (it applies to both the initial purchase and when you move your horse). For less complex transitions, the principles are still

---

*   There are some professionals in the horse world who are not terribly introspective. When sharing constructive feedback with them, you may be met with defensiveness and even hostility. As you learn the personalities in your team, you will get better at knowing the best way to get your message communicated. But calmly and clearly walking through the facts while you presume positive intent on their part will help the process.

the same. Though I have rarely gotten every step of this right in the sequence below, this is my view of an optimal communication protocol:

1. **Confirm the new team member you've selected is available.** Confirm one final time that your new team member, be they a veterinarian, a farrier, or whichever role, is available and keen to be part of your horse's team. This should not be a guaranteed promise to switch to them, but there should be a 95 percent probability that you will do so.

2. **Inform the current team member.** This is the discussion where you share that you plan to make a change. When you share your reasons, none of it should be a surprise to the current team member. They might be surprised you have decided to replace them, but they should have previously heard your complaints and had a chance to rectify things. The reason to not commit 100 percent to the potential new team member (see the prior step) is that it is possible the current team member will tell you something in this discussion that changes your mind. You may have missed something in prior discussions, or they may not have shared it well or at all. Regardless, leave the possibility open for reconciliation if you are presented with truly new and viable information.

   » **If you decide not to switch…circle back immediately with the selected new team member.** Be respectful of the person to whom you gave that 95 percent assurance that you would be switching to them. Call them immediately and let them know you are grateful for their time, advise them that you have decided to stay with the current team member, and share that you hope that you can call them in the future if needed.

   » If you confirm you will be switching…continue with the steps below.

3. **Prepare a transition plan.** This can be as simple as a text to both current and new team members, or it may be a longer email or document with

all the details. A simple plan should at least include the following:

» **Background information:** I would usually call this a "briefing pack," but that presumes a ton of details and pages which are not necessarily required. At a minimum, you should document anything relevant for the new team member, so they are positioned to do their job well. If they are a veterinarian, it may include lots of test results and visit summaries. If they are a massage therapist, it may just be a simple statement such as, "My horse loves massage but seems to hate acupuncture," and/or "Has historically been very tight on his right side." You get the point. Even if you don't write it up, at least do it verbally.

» **Time for team members to chat:** This is not done frequently enough. Set up a time for the current and new team members to chat. If you want to be part of the conversation, ask for that; but make sure it happens even if the logistics of your being involved prove too challenging. This is what provides the insight behind anything in the "background information." It also sets the stage for the new team member to feel free to call with questions (for example, if they are a farrier, calling to ask if a certain kind of pad and shoe combination was ever tried).

» **Key transition dates:** Be clear on the dates to ensure nothing "falls through the cracks" in the transition. This of course includes the date of last interaction with the current team member, and the date of first interaction with the new team member.

» **Billing details confirmation:** Make sure you close out any open bills with the current team member. Also make sure the new team member, either via them directly or their office, has all your billing details to ensure you start off correctly.

4. **Execute the transition plan.** It is then your job to manage the plan. Make sure nothing gets dropped, especially when it could impact the health of your horse.

Do Right by Your Care Team—You Cannot Do This Without Them

Above I share detailed thoughts on how to change team members when necessary because it can be very complicated. So complicated that people frequently put it off far longer than might be best for their horse. That aside, however, the primary takeaway is that no horse owner can take proper care of their horse without a care team. That is why this chapter starts with the statement, "Building and managing the best possible horse care team you can find is job one."

Accordingly, you should do everything in your power to set up every one of your care team members for success and keep them happy supporting your horse and you. A good friend recently had to call in several favors to help a sick horse late one evening. Because she had been a consistently proactive, friendly, organized, punctual, efficient client and had paid her bills on time for many years, her care team members not only responded immediately but some tapped into their own networks for backup plans to make sure the whole complex plan came together.

You'll notice money is the last thing in that list of positive attributes. I share numerous times in this book that paying your bills on time is important, but that is really table stakes. To give you a more complete sense of what I mean, here are some more details:

- **Be proactive.** Make your plans early whenever possible. Other than emergencies, you should be able to get on every single care team member's schedule well in advance. Also, ensure the care team member's office has all of your horse's and your details, including, where applicable, a credit card they can run automatically.
- **Be friendly.** First off, treat every member of your care team's office as professionally and courteously as you do the care team member (I am sad I had to write this part, but I have heard terrible stories…do not be that

person). If a care team member shows up one day uncharacteristically late, stressed, and grumpy, try to make their day better. That might mean just helping them get on their way as fast as possible, or it might mean a bit of levity would help. It is not your job to fix every bad situation, but try to be a net positive.

- **Be organized.** If your horse needs to be ready in a certain way (not ridden, ready to be ridden, groomed, fully bathed, and so on) or you need to be ready (dressed to ride, with a list of prior treatments, and so on), get that done in advance. If your barn is handling anything for you, it is your job to communicate rather than make assumptions.

- **Be punctual.** When the care team member's truck comes through the gate at the barn, everything should be all set. That is far too late a time so say, "Better go get my muddy horse from the farthest paddock."

- **Be efficient.** If you are fully organized per above, you should be set up to be efficient. Then you need to execute. Be present and responsive—rather than distracted—whenever you are working with someone on your care team. If you both have time to chat, that's fantastic. Otherwise, remember they are on a professional schedule and also have a personal life they might like to get to.

- **Pay your bills on time.** Pay in advance, immediately, quickly, or at least on time. As mentioned on page 20, if you might be late for any reason, tell your team member in advance and articulate your plan for making it right.

That's it. Easy peasy. You will remember that early in this book, on page 8, I shared that I don't always do the best job at following my own advice. Many times I have failed at one or more of the items above. When that happens, I endeavor to acknowledge my mistake, apologize, and make a plan to do better next time. So my final recommendation: set your intention to do right by your care team, do the best you can, make it right when you err, and get better over time.

Chapter Seven

Be the Best Advocate and Partner Possible, for Your Horse

Grow into the Myriad of Roles You Play for Your Horse

Gigi Goes to Ocala

I sat in a beautiful conference room with pictures of horses around the room. My horse, Gigi, was at an equine hospital for a CT scan of her head. After weeks of odd symptoms along with inconclusive X-rays and diagnostics, this was the next step. At that time, Ocala had the best CT equipment in the area. And so, I had put Gigi on a truck for the 4-hour trip north. I had gone in the night before during visiting hours to groom her and tell her this was an easy one, just standing sedation required (less stressful and dangerous than general anesthesia).

I felt relaxed, knowing that I had done and was doing everything I could to ensure Gigi was okay. I had questioned vets, trainers, and friends. I had researched everything about her symptoms and the possible diagnostics. I had used the "kitchen sink" approach on testing for anything systemic, going beyond what any of the professionals suggested. I had also written up a 600-word briefing document for her new care team up here in Ocala to ensure nothing was forgotten. And I was there with her that day.

Build up Your Capabilities over Time

Decades ago, when I started with horses, I would not have been able to do any of the tasks involved in my story above: think critically about her symptoms, mood, and energy in recent weeks (both the particulars and the patterns); talk thoughtfully and regularly with multiple types of medical professionals; brainstorm with my trainers and horsey friends; second-guess all the professionals involved to ensure Gigi was getting the best care; arrange and manage all medical care; arrange and manage all shipping; give her ulcer-preventative medication for the short trip (yup, it's a skill); and communicate comprehensively with the entire team, including looping in her dentist in case there was a tooth involved in her situation.

My goal in this chapter is to get you to this more competent and impactful level faster. In the early days, I want you to be an expert at how to lean on your full care team (note: this includes asking lots and lots of questions). As you learn, I want to give you the tools to be a stronger and better orchestrator of that care team (note: this includes having your own opinions while you still ask lots and lots of questions). Being an "owner" starts off seemingly easy. But in meeting each question or challenge that comes with the care of your horse, you eventually become a beautiful blend of guardian, protector, advocate, champion, friend, partner, financier, and mom or dad.

Document a "Horse Care Plan"

Who is responsible for remembering vaccinations, farrier visits, and vet appointments? How many times a day will there be eyes on your horse to notice if he has anything new that needs attention? (Horsey insight: horses can hurt themselves in the space of two minutes even if people are watching, let alone unsupervised for hours in a stall or turnout.) Who keeps track of whether your horse was exercised, or missed three days in a row due to weather and thus might be a lunatic next time you get on him?

Okay, I am a total geek and love templates. You may not actually need to document a formal Horse Care Plan, but there is a template on page 218 if you do. But I promise you this: even if you only print out the template and go through it verbally with your trainer and barn manager, you will be happy you did. You will learn about how they run the barn. You will eliminate many—hopefully most— surprises. And you will know when you should intervene, and when you should leave them to do their jobs.

Open communication is a good thing. But even better is an actual plan (expectations, roles, responsibilities, timing, cost, everything) supplemented by open communication.

Engage Consciously with Your Horse Care Team... Trust, Yet Verify

One of the biggest challenges when you are responsible for a horse is balancing how much to be actively involved while also necessarily trusting the team you have built and their respective systems (how they run the barn or their business generally). Whether you have chosen to essentially "outsource" the horse care responsibilities or do most of it yourself, it always takes a team to ensure things go smoothly. To engage consciously with your team, you should establish a Horse Care Plan, set an intention for all your interactions, presume positive intent from every party, and, if something doesn't feel right, trust your gut and get to the bottom of the situation. You are responsible for the health and welfare of your horse. If you are being reasonable when engaging with your care team and offend a human in the process, you need to get over that. And tell the human, kindly and perhaps with an apology, they need to let it go as well (because horses come first).

You Have a Right to Ask Questions, and a Responsibility
to Stay on Top of Things

I was once told by a fancy trainer that I shouldn't criticize a fancy vet as I had said I would. I ignored the trainer and communicated my perspective to the vet with logic and without emotion. The fancy vet loved talking to an owner that wanted to know the details and didn't automatically want to treat (read: inject) the horse to get him back in the ring ASAP. My priorities were clear from that point forward (horse health and longevity are #1) and both the vet and trainer remained trusted partners in my horse care team for years.

On the heels of that positive story where I stood my ground and did right by my horse (and everyone got along), I'll share a story of which I am less proud. This story is why I add "verify" to the title of this section. When traveling internationally for many years, I would sometimes be gone for weeks at a time. I checked in periodically but generally assumed my barn was exercising my horse sufficiently. At some point in this period, I did not call regularly enough to check on how it was going—this was in the early days of texting. It took a friend at the barn who let me know they thought my horse was barely getting exercised. Was he cared for and turned out daily? Yes. Was he worked sufficiently to stay appropriately fit? No.

Luckily the horse was not fat, though perhaps a bit soft, and nothing terrible happened. But I learned the hard way that when you are not able to be there, you must work harder to be a good advocate for your horse. I also learned that having trustworthy friends in the barn is priceless—not the nosey types who love to create drama for drama's sake, but people who are like aunts and uncles to your horse. They are part of your team. And you are part of theirs. Return the favor.

Trainer, Barn Manager, and Barn Staff

As discussed in the section starting on page 115, every barn has a unique culture, level of professionalism, and way of working. In a barn with an open culture and a high level of professionalism, you will find it easy to ask for help, make requests, ask why something happened the way it did, and generally have adult conversations related to the care of your horse. Also, when the professionalism is high, you will see well-qualified staff with a consistent way of working, one that keeps the barn moving and keeps daily life for your horse calm and predictable.

Questions you should be able to ask without offending anyone:

- I noticed both of my horse's water buckets are empty. I've never noticed this before, so could you find out what happened this time and see how we best prevent it in the future?
- I noticed a small cut on my horse's left hind pastern. Did anyone in the barn notice if that was there yesterday when I wasn't here? What should we, me included, be doing to treat it? Is it okay to still ride him, since there is no swelling or heat, or should I give him some time off? Do we need to call the vet, or are you not that worried about it? If nobody noticed it, can we talk about how regularly he has eyes on him sufficient to notice such a thing?

Questions you should be prepared to answer without being offended:

- We have been using an extra blanket for your horse because you don't have one of [insert blanket specification here] weight. But one of the school horses needs that blanket now, so will you buy one for your horse?
- I noticed you don't spend much time warming up or cooling down your horse. It really is important that you do so, and I'm happy to discuss the best approach.
- I know money is tight, but given your horse has had colic in the past, it is vital that he is on [insert supplement or feed or medication here]. If it's easier for you, we will order it, make sure he gets it every day, and add it to your bill.
- I would like to receive your monthly bill payments by the 5th of each month; it helps massively with cash flow to pay our dedicated staff. Does that work? We're happy to send out text reminders if that helps. Thank you.

A Special Note on Grooms

As a newcomer, you will rely on all the professionals in your barn, not least of whom are the grooms. Even if you get your own horse ready to ride, as I would encourage you to do with supervision, most likely it will be grooms who do almost everything besides riding (though many ride as well). If you are at a smaller barn, every one of the staff members is a groom for part of their day. In a larger barn, the roles are more segmented.

Grooms Know Your Horse Better than You Do

Depending on your barn and your arrangement, the grooms may be responsible for the following types of tasks, all of which involve being with and caring for your equine athlete:

- General care (water, hay, feed, supplement, blanket, mask, muck, turnout, and so on).
- Grooming (bathe, brush, clip, tack up, untack, and so on).
- Exercising (hand walk, lunge, hack, and so on).
- Medical care (bandaging, applying medication…whatever they are authorized to do).
- Event preparation (everything needed to pack, move, set up, and break down for away shows).
- Administrative (ordering supplies, hay, shavings, feed, supplements, and so on).
- Observing and alerting (noticing anything amiss and communicating it to the right people).
- Loving (yes, they love horses too).

Grooms Have a Tough Job with Insufficient Recognition

With that range of potential responsibilities, one would think that grooms would be recognized for their vital role in the horse community. In some places, they are.

And certain institutions are trying to make a difference. But generally, it is a difficult job (long hours, crazy clients, exacting expectations, lots of surprises, sometimes silly travel, often stupid early mornings, and so much more) and they remain what I consider the silent unacknowledged glue that holds the horse world together.

Treat grooms as the respected members of the care team that they are. Be in awe of them. Perhaps even be a bit jealous of them, given all the beautiful time they get to spend with your horse. And thank them, in whatever way and however frequently you can.

Farrier

Questions you should be able to ask without offending anyone:

- Will you tell me what you think of my horse's feet? What do you think of the condition of his hooves? Do you think he needs any supplements?
- Would you look at these X-rays of my horse's feet, to help you decide the best shoeing approach for him?
- My vet suggested a certain kind of shoeing; would you talk with them to come up with a joint plan on what is best for him? I'd love to be on the call, but it's more important that you all talk and one of you let me know the plan.

Questions you should be prepared to answer without being offended:

- I haven't seen any improvement in your horse's hoof condition. Have you been giving him the supplement and using the treatment I suggested?
- I would like to receive payment for my services within a week of doing your horse's shoes. Does that work? It helps me a lot. Thank you.

Veterinarians (General, Soundness, Specialist)

Questions you should be able to ask without offending anyone:

- How far apart do you like to give your vaccinations? I know some of them are combined, but I would prefer to space them out as much as possible.
- Will you send me the X-rays?

- I don't see what you're talking about with his right front being off; can you tell me what you're seeing? Eventually I hope to develop a better eye for these things.
- Would you write up a formal pre-purchase exam report with everything you saw and your recommendations? It will give me a helpful baseline from which to manage his care going forward.

Questions you should be prepared to answer without being offended:
- Did you, or someone on the barn staff, use the anti-fungal shampoo twice a day like we talked about when I was here last week?
- I would like to receive payment for my services within a week from when we send out the bills. Does that work? It helps my practice a lot. Thank you.

A Special Note on Veterinarians

When you meet your first equine veterinarian, you will rightly be amazed by their intellect, perception, and caring rigor. Most have excellent stall-side manners if you are curious and attentive, though some can be a bit gruff. There are two main things I want to relay so you do not join this party unawares.

- **We do not have enough equine veterinarians, and the pipeline is dwindling.** There has been a trend in recent years of there simply not being enough equine veterinarians. It is one of the most prestigious degrees, but the numbers indicate it has become less appealing as a vocation. This leads to overload on the existing veterinarians. The stresses of the pandemic only made things worse, with the addition of clients being even more demanding, and indeed rude. Many veterinarians had to send out mass communications outlining what types of behavior were not acceptable when dealing with practice staff. You or I are not going to solve the equine veterinarian availability problem, but decent human behavior might make their workplace a little more appealing (see the section starting on page 20 for my take on such good practices).

- **Equine veterinarians care deeply about horses and owners, but they do not run a charity.** This happens to small animal veterinary practices as well, but there seems to be something about emergency medical costs that makes some horse owners believe they can demand services they cannot afford. This book covers how to budget for most eventualities and what you might consider for insurance. If you ignore all of that and end up with a horse for whom you cannot afford the right medical care (either out-of-pocket or with the support of insurance you purchased), that is neither the fault nor responsibility of the veterinarian on call. You can bring up the idea of a potential payment plan or other creative ideas, but you do not have a right to demand thousands (or tens of thousands) of dollars of services with a poor track record of paying your bill.

Everyone has stories about veterinarians who were flexible and many who went quite far trying to be helpful in this regard, and that is both gracious and up to them. As with every expenditure that horses come with, whatever your horse needs is your responsibility. In extreme circumstances of sudden hardship, there are organizations who might have the bandwidth to help—please seek those out with the help of your barn if you are ever in this situation. But as a general matter—and again, this applies to every equine service provider—do whatever you need to do to be prepared to pay your bills immediately or at the latest by the due date. And when something unusual comes up, let them know you might be late so they can plan properly.

Document Everything in Trackers

Are we up to date on Coggins and vaccinations? How many times have we treated his hocks, and when was the last time? Your horse's feet look long…when was he last shod? Who will do the health certificate for the upcoming trip? How does your horse respond to acupuncture…is he okay with it and has it helped in the past? When did we start that supplement for his coat? How long has he been on the ulcer treatment?

If you live and breathe horses, you may well be able to answer these questions off the top of your head. I am better at doing that now than I was many years ago, but I still prefer to document things along the way whenever possible. The Horse Care Tracker starting on page 221 and the Horse Exercise Tracker starting on page 223 are approaches you can use. Some barns have a daily log for such things; that's a great source of information that you can double-check, but I like having my own summary for my horses.

Think Holistically, as Everything You Do with Horses Interrelates

This point cannot be overstated. One of your jobs as the CEO of your horse's life is to pay attention to the top-down view (everything going on in their lives) in addition to the bottom-up view (the details of what exactly is happening). Even when you don't think you're doing anything wrong, you might be. So in your early days with horses, inform every professional of what is going on with your horse—this is why there is a Horse Care Tracker starting on page 221. This is a great tool to share a comprehensive view of your horse's care—and make sure their planned treatment is safe. Safe not just in a "this always works" way, but in this way: "This makes the most sense for your horse, considering everything we know about his medical history, his current health and demeanor, and his most recent treatments."

As you mature in your role as advocate, you will develop and hold the line on principles that make sense to you. A few of my key principles are listed below— you will add more to your own list over time.

- **Be cautious with your vaccinations.** Spread out the necessary vaccinations, even if it means more trips from the vet (and even if the vet or barn finds it less convenient for their schedule). Don't do vaccinations near anything stressful (travel, showing, shoeing); for some horses, the internal and external stress can culminate in negative health effects.

- **Be calculated with any care changes.** Adjust any feed or supplements in a slow and methodical manner. Keep everything the same when at a show, traveling, or in any situation where a horse may have additional stress; don't introduce new treatments for the first time when the horse is already under stress.

- **Get forensic about any significant changes.** For any decisions of consequence (care changes, shoeing changes, medical treatments, *all. of. it.*), I work very hard to verify what I am being told. These are the typical questions, in progressively complex order: What precisely are we trying to fix? Why do we need to do anything? What is it you are proposing, and when? How do you know that works? What are the risks generally? What are the risks for my horse given he has a diagnosis of ABC and a history of XYZ? What are the most common alternatives, and their relative risks? Are there cheaper (reasonably or equally effective) alternatives? Are there more natural (reasonably or equally effective) alternatives? And (though this is sadly rare in the horse world) are there current independent scientific studies on the topic—not just ones published by the manufacturer?

- **Where possible and appropriate, change one thing at a time.** Especially when you are working through a fitness, soundness, health, or behavioral challenge, it is often helpful to methodically adjust in a stepwise manner. This approach helps you understand what helped and what didn't, which makes it easier to find long-term solutions and to avoid, for example, giving umpteen supplements because you added five at the same time and things got better, and now you don't know which supplement was the key. If a situation is critical, you may not have the luxury of going slow. And sometimes the answer is a combination of things. Just make it a principle that you are trying to get to both the root of the problem and the core elements of the solution.

Even if you have predominantly outsourced the care role for your horse to your barn and trainer (as stated previously, this is a reasonable model in many situations), you still can ask some basics and make sure they have good answers: *Why? What? When? How? Alternatives? Risks?* I'm not saying you need to ask questions about everything, but it's rare that a change doesn't have an implication for your horse. These are sensitive creatures of habit, and they are hunted animals. They find comfort in patterns, such that shifts in the logistics of care ("Let's change when we do night check!") can have an impact on them, let alone adjustments to the care itself ("Let's try this new [supplement/medical treatment/ type of shoe/*ad infinitum*] I just saw on Instagram, promoted by [famous horse person XYZ]!").

Keep Horses Out of Dangerous Situations, Yet Be Prepared for Emergencies

If you are new to horses, you will be surprised at the speed with which a situation can go from seemingly innocuous to downright dangerous.

- Your horse has always stood still when you pick his feet in the stall. So, one time, you don't put the halter on him nor close the door tight while you clean his feet; and this time, rather than standing still, he trots himself out of the stall and goes frolicking into the indoor arena where a jumping lesson is underway. (Yes, I did this—my horse was very proud of himself— and, yes, I remain grateful that no horses or people were harmed.)
- Your horse has gotten on and off trailers dozens of times without a care in the world, but this time something spooks him and you don't have good enough hold of him; he steps off the back ramp sideways and scrapes his leg badly.
- The stories are truly endless.

There are many quality books covering horsemanship that focus on horse (and rider) safety. This quick list of rules does not even come close to covering the topic, but it's a start. My main objective is to scare you so you take this seriously, continually learn, and ask how to do better for the safety of your horse.

- Listen to everything your trainer, barn manager, or barn staff tell you to do and not do when it comes to safety. If they give you conflicting advice, ask them to clarify.
- Stay off your phone anytime being distracted could create a problem or slow your response time—in the early days, this might mean leaving your phone in your car when you are at the barn.
- Always have a halter or bridle on your horse when outside the stall or turnout, and check your barn protocol about whether horses wear halters in turnout.
- When you go in a stall, fully close the door behind you before you put on his halter—remember my story above where I got this very wrong and my halter-less horse went for a frolic in the indoor arena in the middle of a jumping lesson.
- Double-check that you have secured the stall door and turnout gate when you are the last to leave your horse there. Check it multiple times if you need to, but this rule is a really simple way to keep things safe. And don't kid yourself that you will just not latch the stall door for "2 seconds to get a brush"...latch it *every* time, and you won't run the risk of getting distracted.
- Though it might seem cute, don't let two horses meet by touching noses if you don't know that they already get along. Even a friendly squeal and slight rear can create a very dangerous situation.
- Be aware of and in tune with your surroundings at all times. If the manure truck is pulling in and you were about to get on a lesson horse, maybe wait, or at least ask someone whether this horse will be bothered by the loud manure removal equipment.

- If a horse is new to you, lock the gate when you lunge him the first few times. We recently bought one that turned out to be a runner. At a show, he got away from the person lungeing him, ran off the show grounds, and (seriously) ended up at the local pub. He apparently did not order a beer, but we believe if he had had more time there, someone would have given him one. No horses or humans were hurt, but it was terrifying nonetheless.
- *Ad infinitum.*

Remember, you are not only protecting your horse. You are also protecting all the other horses by not creating or enabling a dangerous situation with your horse.

Connect with Your Horse in Every Way You Know How

In the section starting on page 35, I shared the value of thinking through, and periodically revisiting, your objectives in your relationship with your horse. Whether you want to simply trail ride or are keen to compete, your partnership with your horse starts with your connection, your bond. Your job in this relationship is to be calm, patient, consistent, observant, empathetic, vigilant, and caring. Your horse's job is to be a horse. On page 19, I shared my view of horse rights and human responsibilities. On page 151, I shared all the roles you play for your own horse. You. Are. Their. Person.

Here, I bring up Pony Club again because everyone should take advantage of it if there is one near you (https://www.ponyclub.org). They offer programs for adults in some areas. Nothing can replace this type of structured, hands-on learning. Not a book. Not even this fine book. If you're an adult, check your ego at the door and start with the basics. Buy all the manuals, pore through the details, and show up to learn. They will cover all the basics about parts of the horse, grooming, care, safety, and eventually riding. This book helps you know what you're getting into, so you are prepared to do right by the horses in your life. Pony Club actually teaches you about horses and physically how to do right by them. If you are reading this for your child, consider 4-H as well.

Though the primary theme of this book is how to do right by horses, I share here my thoughts for how that can translate into a better bond with your horse. There are whole books on this topic written by people more skilled than me, but these ideas certainly might help.

- Calm down, and slow down.
- Listen, and then listen with more focus.
- Watch, and then watch with a soft eye.
- Let it go when now is not the time.
- Let it go when today is not the day.
- Remember whatever you did that your horse seemed to appreciate. Do that more.
- Tell him he is perfect. Mean it (that means eliminate the "he's perfect *except for XYZ*" part that might pop into your brain) and tell him every day.
- Help him grow. He is perfect, but he can develop into a more evolved state of perfect. Just like you.
- Keep your promises.
  - » I have a social contract with my horse Gigi that at the end of our ride we always trot on a loose rein; I let her stretch as low as she likes, nose to the ground if that's what feels good to her. After that final trot, I never re-start work. My view is she deserves the clear indicator of a job well done. Would she start working again if I asked? Probably. I see no reason to ask her.

Be Thoughtful about End-of-Life Care

Similar to the section starting on page 65, where I brought up retirement as a topic fairly early in that chapter, here I want to discuss how we care for horses into retirement, in their final years, and up to and including that final day. I am not an expert on this topic, but I believe helping you think about the topic is worthwhile even if I cannot (and indeed should not) prescribe answers.

Consider Quality-of-Life Factors with Aging Horses

There are beautiful stories of aging horses who defy the odds and are moving around their spaces with the ease of a much younger horse, and others who live life to the fullest and quietly pass in their sleep. These are outcomes to pray for, but not to plan for.

Aging horse bodies do what aging bodies tend to do. They get creaky and gray almost certainly, and then anything that can go wrong simply might go wrong. You need to be careful with aging horses' environments so as not to increase a risk of falling (on ice, for example) as their four legs don't react quite as quickly and even a slip could have disastrous effects. But generally, the horse will tell you by his habits, patterns, moods, and movements how he is doing. Barring sudden trauma leading to a painful existence that everyone, the horse included, agrees should not continue, the answer is rarely obvious.

I Would Rather Help My Horse Go a Day Too Early Than a Minute Too Late

All the horse people are going to pounce on this tagline…"Of course! That's what we all want, but how do you *know* when that moment is?!?" Aside from experts telling you that there is no hope and it's only a painful downhill from here, you don't get to know the exact moment. As brutal as this seems, first start by asking yourself these two questions:

- Do you understand that horses can live a long happy life beyond their working years, especially when you support them in that endeavor?
- Do you understand what a bad end looks like for a horse, and how being unprepared (if not slightly proactive) can lead to unnecessary suffering?

With that backdrop, my goal here is to help you think about the journey to having to make decisions regarding end-of-life care for your horse. Here are some questions I ask myself:

- Does he have a good quality of life right now? If I think so, what is the evidence of that in his body, behavior, and mood? Could it be better in any way?
- Are there any current signs of aging? What are they and are they typical of his age?
- What historical medical issues (lameness, illness, and so on) might start to show up again as he ages, and can I help prevent that from happening or getting worse, even a bit?
- Considering both his physical and emotional state, is his current environment one that is healthy for him as he ages? Are there better reasonable alternatives, and is it worth the risk of moving him?
- Do all the people who interact with him know him well enough to notice if he is degrading slightly over time?
- How is he starting to show signs of age and discomfort, and does he seem to be handling them okay with the support we are giving him?

As a horse starts to show severe signs of age and discomfort, the question remains how to judge when he has had enough or is at imminent risk of suffering acutely or chronically. Talk with your horse friends, your equine veterinarians, your spiritual advisors, and anyone who will help you work it through. You're threading the needle of life here…do right by the horses in your life by thinking it through in advance and standing tall in making the best decision you know how for them every step of the way. And that includes when the time comes that is truly best for him to go, and yet that decision is brutally, horribly, and agonizingly painful for you. Doing right by him in the end is as or more important than at any other time in his life.

Templates
Template: Horse Care Plan

Barn Name	
Registered Name	
Horse USEF #	
Primary Vet	
Date	
Owner	Name, USEF #, and phone #
Authorized for decisions if owner unavailable	Include name, phone #, email (can be trainer)
Trainer	Name, phone #
Barn Manager	Name, phone #
Farrier	Name, phone #
Insurance Contact	Name, phone # (notify if life-threatening)
Insurance Policy #	ok of course to have "n/a" here if not insured

HORSE CARE PLAN CONTINUED

Activity	Notes	Owner	Trainer	Staff
General Care Management				
Feed	Which feed? How much each meal? 2x or 3x/day (some barns do lunch)?			
Supplements	Which supplements?			
Medication in Feed	Which medication in feed?			
Medication/ Treatment	Anything needed on an ongoing basis? Anything special right now?			
Hay	Which type of hay? Pounds/ day and timing?			
Stall Cleaning	How frequent? Include water check?			
Turnout	Time of day? How long? Water in turnout?			
Walker (e.g., treadmill)	Available? How frequent for how long?			
Hand Walk	Available? How frequent for how long?			
Night Check	What time? Include stall picking? Hay? Eyes on horse?			
Worming	How frequently? Replace with fecal check on what frequency?			
GastroGuard	Needed for travel or other situations?			
Engaging Outside Horse Care Team				
Farrier				
Veterinarian— Primary				
Veterinarian— Soundness	(if different)			

Activity	Notes	Owner	Trainer	Staff
Engaging Outside Horse Care Team (Continued)				
Specialists and Surgeons				
Other Medical				
Dentist				
Chiropractor				
Acupuncture				
Massage				
Private Parts Cleaning	(Laugh at me if you like for making this a row in my table, but please get this done regularly for your horse by someone who knows what they are doing.)			
General Expectations for #/Week				
Tack Up	Includes bringing in from turnout if applicable, grooming, getting ready.			
Untack	Take care of everything the horse needs after he has been ridden or worked.			
Lesson				
Hack without Lesson				
Training Ride				

Activity	Notes	Owner	Trainer	Staff
General Expectations for #/Week (Continued)				
Hack -by Trainer or -by Staff/Other				
Lunge -regular -with equipment (red rope, and so on)	Clarity on what kind of equipment, bridle vs. halter, length of time, everything.			
Additional for Hard Work/Showing				
Icing?				
Wrapping?				
Magnet therapy?				

Template: Horse Care Tracker

[this will be in landscape orientation]	Typical Frequency (talk to your vet!!)	Jan	Feb	Mar	etc.
Coggins and Vaccinations					
Coggins	Annual				
Flu/Rhino	Every 6 months				
West Nile					
EEE/WEE + Tetanus					
Rabies					
[add or subtract for your geography]					

[this will be in landscape orientation]	Typical Frequency (talk to your vet!!)	Jan	Feb	Mar	etc.
Regular Maintenance					
Farrier	Every 4–6 weeks				
Worming/Fecal	Varies				
Dental	Every 6 months				
Privates Cleaning	2–3x/year				
[add or subtract for your geography]					
Regular Health and Wellness Checks					
General Health, Blood, Weight Check	2–3x/year				
Feed & Supplement Review	2–3x/year				
Soundness Check	2–3x/year				
Special Maintenance					
Special Diagnostics (for example, X-ray, blocking, MRI, CT)	As needed				
Chiropractor	As needed				
Acupuncture	As needed				
Massage	As needed				
Shockwave, Magna-wave/PEMF, Laser	As needed				
Other maintenance (per vet)	With caution				
Other procedures (for example, surgery)	Hopefully never				
[add or subtract for your purposes]					

Template: Horse Exercise Tracker

[Horse Name] [Month]	Turnout	Hand Walk or Lunge	Owner: Lesson or Ride	Barn: School or Hack	Comments
1—Sun					
2—Mon					
3—Tue					
4—Wed					
5—Thu					
6—Fri					
7—Sat					
8—Sun					
9—Mon					
10—Tue					
11—Wed					
12—Thu					
13—Fri					
14—Sat					
[and so on]					

Chapter Eight

Be the Best Horseperson and Barn Member Possible, for Yourself

Be Curious, Intentional, and Grateful to Enhance Your Life with Horses

Do not wish your early days in the horse world away thinking, "I just want to get past all this beginner stuff and be as good as XYZ." Whether you are a "newcomer" as a rider or as a parent, remember that joining this world as an adult has advantages. You know yourself, you have agency and freedom, and you can make every minute count and remember it all. Revel in that.

Indeed, let the whole experience wash over you. Be curious and attentive to everything about the horse world, horses and horse people included. Be intentional, thoughtful, and discerning about how you spend your time, energy, passion, and money as you work through each step of the journey. And, perhaps most importantly, be grateful for every moment, and for the chance to experience the awe and wonder of horses as only your beginner's eyes, body, and soul can. The good times and the hard times will teach you to be a better human; look at all the lessons that way if you can. You will not always be a newcomer, but you can use your newcomer time to grow up into the type of caring seasoned horse person, and indeed human, you admire.

Develop a Positive Bond and Relationship with Your Horse

This message from the prior chapter bears repeating. Whether you are riding a different lesson horse each week or have your own horse, connecting in the most meaningful way possible with each horse is the point of this whole enterprise. To start thinking about how to bond with your horse, or any horse, I encourage you to re-read the section starting on page 19 on your responsibilities and the horse's rights, especially these rights:

Subset of "The Horse's Rights" from page 19

3. *To be recognized as his own being—with feelings and quirks, likes and dislikes, strengths and weaknesses, and good days and bad days (yes, just like us).*

4. *To be in a job that suits his body, character, age, and natural abilities (know that sometimes this implies he might be best suited to be a magnificent lawn ornament).*

Starting with this paradigm goes a long way to developing the bond and relationship you desire. Fighting reality never works, especially with horses. But being in sync with your horse and learning how to better listen and communicate will bring you along the journey. I am not a horse whisperer, but I work every day to listen, sense, and watch so that I have a better chance of understanding and communicating with my horse. I am not a trainer, but I try my best to be consistent and responsive in all my interactions with my horse, including riding, so that at a minimum I do not untrain him in unhelpful ways.

In the Resources section starting on page 260, I provide a list of the books, magazines, and online sources (blogs and podcasts) that I have found helpful when working on my relationship with my horse. Given my own newbie status ("only" 25 years in the horse world and almost all as a weekend warrior), I hope you will agree that it is better to learn from the masters on the topic of bonding, connecting, and communicating with your horse, along with horsemanship and how to ride.

Build a Productive Relationship with Your Barn and Trainer

As a newcomer, you will rely heavily on your chosen professionals when you are working with your horse and riding. Though it is always helpful to chat with other horse people about your horsemanship, it is your trainer who will be helping you make your entry into the world of horses a success. Given the role they play in this endeavor is critical, a healthy and productive working relationship is vital.

As with every relationship, everyone must act honestly, transparently, and ethically for the thing to work. A summary of the desires on either side of the relationship:

Category	You want your trainer to...	Your trainer wants you to...
Respect	Respect your objectives, constraints, time, and money; value you and your horse as important clients and members of the barn; and presume you are operating with positive intent.	Respect their business model, constraints, time, and money; value them for their efforts and contributions to your horse journey; and presume they are operating with positive intent.
Honesty	Be honest about your riding and your horse, and their own business priorities where they might impact you.	Be clear and honest about your overall situation as it pertains to horses, along with your objectives and constraints.
Empathy	Understand you and your horse, and remember your underlying fears/weaknesses/stressors when you have shared or showed them.	Understand them, and be understanding when things go awry (as they can do in the horse world, even with best intentions and efforts).

Category	You want your trainer to...	Your trainer wants you to...
Communication	Communicate how to improve your horsemanship and riding in ways that you can understand, and be responsive when you need help.	Pay attention in lessons (and around the barn), endeavor to remember what they told you previously, and communicate what you don't understand so they can help.
Integrity	Raise issues and conflicts with you directly (instead of generating gossip) as soon as they know about them, and own it when they get things wrong.	Raise issues with them directly (instead of generating gossip) when you have them, and own it when you get things wrong.
Diligence	Uphold their horse care responsibilities, be on time for all things possible, plan events and shows well in advance, and be clear and consistent on costs and billing.	Uphold your horse care responsibilities, be on time for all things possible, uphold your commitments to join events and shows, and pay your bills on time.
Professionalism	Run a professional barn and staff and be a positive role model for a no-drama barn.	Be courteous and professional to the entire staff and generally be a positive—instead of drama-inspiring—member of the barn.

With that introduction, a few more of these factors supporting a positive working relationship merit more discussion.

Get Aligned on Your Objectives and Monitor Your Riding Progress Regularly

When you are first starting, getting aligned on objectives may be one of the easier tasks. You want to learn about horses, begin to ride, and be safe in doing all of it. And besides, you discussed your overall objectives when you were picking the barn and trainer (see the section starting on page 35 if that sounds unfamiliar).

Once you have some time in the barn and saddle under your proverbial belt, then comes the time for more thorough conversations.

Certain sports have methodical ways to track your evolving proficiency. As best I know, horsemanship and riding only have one internationally common way of doing that, and it is—bringing it up again—Pony Club. I never participated in Pony Club, and I understand there is some snobbery afoot about it—I care little about snobbery and a lot about what works. Having bought the Pony Club manuals that define their curriculum and talked to a few people who went through it, the structure and objective proficiency monitoring is fabulous to me. Though horseback riding can be more art than science at times, I still think a disciplined methodology is helpful, at least to those of us who like such things.

On an annual-ish basis, it is healthy to sit down with your trainer, and key assistants if appropriate, to review any updates to your riding objectives, showing goals if applicable, general circumstances, and horse situation. This is also a good time to weave in any feedback about what you love so far and what would make things better for you. This is not the time to blindside your trainer with major issues, just an opening for any minor things that might come up naturally in a "sit down" (read: neither of you riding or taking care of a horse at the time) conversation. Perhaps a few times a year, then, you could have a healthy check-in to make sure things are on track, share a new objective, or open up about anything top of mind.

On an almost daily basis, you should be using your interactions with all the professionals around you (trainers, barn management, grooms) to solicit constructive feedback. Though trainers will tell you what they want you to work on in a lesson, it is appropriate to ask whether they think you've progressed on any point of improvement needed in your riding or horsemanship.

Uphold Your Responsibilities on Time, Attention, and Money

The title of this section is really all you need to remember. This may be "just" a hobby to you, and certainly sometimes things happen that impact your ability to uphold your responsibilities. However, the best way to build a productive relationship with your barn is to fulfill your responsibilities fully and consistently as near to 100 percent of the time as possible.

- **Time:** A barn runs on a schedule. Know the hours they are open and abide by them unless there is a medical issue. When you have a lesson, be tacked up and ready to get on your horse at lesson start time. Only when you are capable and allowed to ride alone, you might also consider coming a bit early to have a longer warmup. But check with your trainer, as sometimes overlapping with an earlier lesson time is unhelpful.
- **Attention:** Pay attention to your horse (watch for bumps or scrapes, mood shifts, responsiveness when riding, and so on), your trainer (listen to what they're saying, make sure you understand), your peers (if you are riding, it is your job to not run into anybody), your body (check your strength, balance, breath, mood, and so on), and your gear (all the things you need to take care of and ride your horse). When you're new, it will seem overwhelming. Once you have practice, it will become more natural. In the early days, ask lots of questions, and pay attention as much as possible.
- **Money:** The simplest point here is to pay all your bills on time, every time, to everyone (see the long list of financial responsibilities starting on page 64). If every member of a barn did this, things would run a lot more smoothly. Nobody wants to chase you for money; it's not fun. And if you know you will be late, talk about it with the person you owe money to. It's still not great, but at least they can try to plan around the negative impact to their cash flow. When you commit to something, ranging from a lesson to a show, know that if you back out at the last minute, you are still likely responsible for most, if not all, of your original financial commitment.

Be a Good Member of the Barn

This one is hilarious to write about, as it is akin to saying, "Be a good human." There are thousands of books on that topic, and I won't attempt to synthesize them. But here is an attempt at a few principles to help you be a positive, constructive, and healthy part of your barn community.

- **Take care of your horse.** This remains job #1, so abide by everything below as long as it doesn't conflict with caring for your horse.

- **Say something if you see anything wrong with any horse.** Even if you are incorrect about something being amiss—you will make mistakes in the early days, and likely forever—it is far better to say, "Is this right?" than to let it go and have something bad happen. Empty water bucket, stall door open, swollen leg, fly mask off one ear, blanket hanging mostly off the horse in turnout, anything…make a query to a responsible person.

- **Mind your own business.** Unless horse or rider safety is in question (see prior point), stay out of whatever is going on in the barn that you might find intriguing. This goes for junior meltdowns, terrible lesson happenings, a ridiculous choice in horse boot color, a dreadful mistake someone made in the ring…all of it. You have your values, other people have theirs. Let it be.

- **Be kind to all the humans.** All. Of. Them. Trainers, barn staff, grooms, farriers, vets, other riders, moms of other riders, visiting uncles of other riders, UPS delivery person, snow-plow person, hay-delivery person…everyone. Even in a small barn, you will meet a lot of people. 99 percent of them are hard-working people who love horses, even if some are a bit tired and jaded. Bond on the strength of that shared love of horses, and let any other concerns go.

- **Be kind to all the horses.** Do not feed horses that are not yours unless you have direct permission from their person, but being present and loving to every horse in the barn is always appreciated.

- **Take care of your stuff.** Keep your gear clean, put your stuff away, and clean up after your horse (including manure, hoof pickings, mane trimmings… all of it). Multiple trainer friends of mine requested repetition here: Put.

Your. Stuff. Away. Sure, we all make mistakes and forget sometimes, but focus on this topic and apologize sincerely when you err.

- **Wait your turn.** If someone is talking to your trainer or barn manager or whomever, wait until they are done and then ask your question. Better yet, signal you want to chat, then walk away to give them some privacy.
- **Wait, and be ready, for your turn in lessons.** When you're in a group lesson, let the trainer finish coaching the prior rider, but also be ready to go as soon as it is your turn. This can be like threading a needle; pay attention to the flow, and you'll get in the groove.
- **Share any barn concerns politely, privately, and early.** Whether you are concerned about how your horse is being cared for or feel you're not making as much progress as you like, you need to raise it politely and directly with your trainer or barn manager. This sounds obvious, but do not add your complaint to the petri dish that is the barn gossip machine. It doesn't solve the problems and only makes it harder for the professionals trying to help you and your horse.

Be Thoughtful about How Far You Extend Your Friendship with Your Trainer

I have developed strong, enduring friendships with multiple trainers, barn staff, and grooms over the years. I have also had relationships that were 90 percent professional, while of course being friendly given the time spent together. There is no one right model, but it is worth thinking about what you think will work best for you.

A few thoughts on the matter that may or may not be obvious:

- The more you make friends, especially to a degree where it feels like family, the more fraught it can become to address professional and business issues when they arise (read: family dysfunction).
- Remember there is always a professional element to the relationship. You

have hired them for their knowledge, skills, and time; yes, you pay them for a service. And for your trainers, you have also hired them to coach you and tell you what to do; the power balance can be delicate.

- Some trainers already require unwavering allegiance to them (see the section starting on page 123) and their barn, so be careful of making them a good friend as well.
- One of the horse world's many joys is debriefing your rides with your trainer and others in your barn, sometimes late into the evening. Especially if you're traveling together for away shows, it is impossible not to evolve your relationship; be conscious of this and decide how far you want to go.

For those of you who are consenting adults, I have no opinion on whether any friendship in the horse world develops into something more significant. That topic belongs in a different book. But read on to the next section, which discusses those in the horse world who are not adults.

Watch Out for Anyone Underage in the Horse World, and Report Suspected Misconduct

Extra caution and diligence must be used in relation to children and juniors in the horse world. If you have a child or are around children in this sport, read on. If you are underage yourself, read on as well. And forgive me this…I am allowing myself two expletives in this entire book and both are in the next sentence: Abuse, of any kind, of minors in sports is serious life-altering shit, and bad shit happens every single day, so pay attention, take nothing for granted, and make every effort not to fool yourself ("Oh, XYZ would *never* do anything inappropriate!" has been said about every perpetrator, or no one would have let them near a minor in the first place). Also see the section on this topic related to being the parent of a horse-mad child, starting on page 250.

In the United States, the U.S. Center for SafeSport was created in 2017 after systemic abuse of minors was exposed and prosecuted shockingly late. Though the sport that made the problem famous was US Women's Gymnastics, every sport with minors involved has the risk of sexual misconduct. And there are so many layers and type of non-sexual misconduct and abuse, it is worth learning more so that you understand the signs and nuances and also know what to do when you notice something. As an adult, you can no longer compete in USEF events if you haven't completed your SafeSport training. SafeSport is not perfect— personally, I worry about non-legal bodies dealing with life-altering charges—but they are working hard on a massively difficult topic. I share here a small part of the resources available online at usef.org/safe-sport.

Report Non-Sexual Misconduct to USEF

USEF handles all reports of non-sexual misconduct, including harassment, hazing, bullying, physical or emotional misconduct, or a violation of the Minor Athlete Abuse Prevention Policies. Non-sexual misconduct may be reported to USEF by submitting an Incident Report Form to usefsafesport@usef.org, or emailing/calling a representative on the Athlete Protection Team.

Report Sexual Misconduct to the U.S. Center for SafeSport

Make a report electronically to the U.S. Center for SafeSport or call 833-5US-SAFE if you have a reasonable suspicion of sexual misconduct such as child sex abuse, non-consensual sexual conduct, sexual harassment, or intimate relationships involving an imbalance of power.

Report Sexual Misconduct to Local Authorities

Contact your local authorities if you have a reasonable suspicion that child sexual abuse or neglect has occurred. All reports of child abuse or sexual assault of a minor must be reported to local authorities and the U.S. Center for Safe-Sport. Reports of abuse not involving a minor should also be reported to local authorities.

If you live in a different country, find the contact information for your local resources working on this issue *before* you need their help. Perpetrators are careful, but they can make mistakes that are noticeable if you have a watchful eye, ear, and sense of energy.

Be Prepared for the Psychological Elements of This Sport

As noted in the section starting on page 3, the vast majority of the physical, emotional, spiritual, and psychological effects of being in the horse world are hugely positive. Your life will never be the same, and almost all of the differences are for the good. Whether you are a new rider as an adult or are supporting your horse-mad child in their dreams, simply knowing the challenges in advance can help. You may or may not find them to be actually challenging. In fact, they can be a constructive part of the learning journey.

Whether you want to compete or not, being with and around horses comes with some unique challenges. And though the physical elements are obvious (being in shape, having good balance and body control), the psychological elements are arguably the biggest drivers behind real progress in your horsemanship and riding. I share here a few things that may be helpful, and if you are keen on the topic, please also read the Resources section starting on page 260 for more detail. I have hardly cracked the psychological game, but I sure do keep trying. It is about all any of us mere mortals can do. And the people who appear to be of the gods in this sport have undoubtedly spent more time than you or me on perfecting their psychological or "mental" program (and, potentially, their emotional and spiritual path as well).

Falling in Love with These Creatures and Potentially Over-Extending Yourself

Falling in love with a sport can lead to making seemingly crazy decisions that impact your relationships, time allocations, and financials. I have elite athlete friends in Boulder who do what I consider to be crazy things (all variety of extreme sports); they love their chosen sports and none of it seems crazy to them. I have non-horsey friends who think what I do with horses is crazy, and yet none of it seems crazy to me.

What is unique about the horse world is that you not only come to love the sport, the feeling, the people, and the whole enterprise, but you also fall in love with these creatures. Sure, an elite mountain biker loves their bike, but it doesn't compare to the love you will have for the horse in your life. You will do anything for him. Not just because you are responsible for him, but because he feeds your soul, and you want to do right by him.

So, that is a very long-winded introduction to the message to be careful with your heart, time, and money, and avoid going so far as to end up unwittingly risking other parts of your life. If you want to change your life priorities, that is of course all good…my caution is to do so consciously, with real thought, and not solely because you get swept up in the moment and struggle to regain normalcy.

Though to date I have "gotten away with it"—meaning I haven't had to take out a loan to make it all work, beyond that 401k loan for my first horse I mentioned earlier, or anything worse—I have faced this challenge repeatedly over the years. When I knew I needed a financial break from showing, I still signed up for the next one because "we did so great in that last class at this show, I just have to keep going!" The examples are many. Even when you are a rigorous budget manager, you are at risk of being swept away. And that is just for yourself. I count the risk as higher for being swept when you have a horse-mad child (one with a puppy-dog look in their eyes when they ask for that next horsey-related thing).

Please review the sections starting on pages 109 and 253 for how to save money in the horse world; if nothing else, it can help you recover when you have made an expensive choice.

Dealing with the Brain-Stem-Level Fear That Riding Can Sometimes Produce

After one horse stopped hard on me a couple times, landing me on the ground or on the jump, I struggled to get my mojo back. We were able to help the horse easily, but I ended up going to a sport psychologist because everything was suddenly scary to me, and I was berating myself for what I judged as silly reactions.

What I learned from that psychologist helped me immensely. In short, when fear is brain-stem-level fear (read: the reptilian brain), all the approaches to resolving it involving higher-order thinking will not work. My telling myself that my fear was silly ("You've jumped plenty of bigger jumps, just get on with it!") was counter-productive. Honoring the fear, rather than belittling myself for it, and using their suggested techniques to work through it was the path to being truly back in the saddle.

This is a dangerous sport. I've hurt myself badly falling off while getting on a horse. I've hurt myself when walking along a seemingly safe area. I've met people recovering from debilitating injuries; some permanent and others partially or fully recoverable. And I've read the stories of those who lost their lives doing the sport they love. So your reptilian brain is not wrong to be concerned. But your mature brain can think about all the things you can do to stay safer, and the low probabilities of those terrible situations; your reptilian brain only knows it is afraid. The fear is real, and it is better to know about it and find the best tactics that help you personally to manage it than to ridicule yourself for having the fear.

Handling the Steps Back and Plateaus in a Sport You Can (Happily!) Never Perfect

I suppose there is no sport where you ever get it all "right," such that you don't need to work on improving anymore. But in some sports—swimming, for example—you will see certain athletes repeatedly and consistently win. With work, they hold on to their top position. The top athletes in the horse world also win or place more regularly than others, but they still have days that are not their days.

A top rider on a top horse might still be eliminated or retire in a round; it just happens in this unique sport where human and horse athletes must both be at their best.

I talk about all that to help you be a bit less frustrated when one of two things happen: A) you go backwards in your riding, and B) you hit a plateau of annoying duration. When you go backwards, the best approach is to honor it and go two steps back to build yourself back up. If you can't do something you used to be able to do at the trot, just do it at the walk—or, better, do whatever your trainer is telling you to do to help get back what used to be solidly in your skillset. Don't berate yourself with, "But I used to be able to do this…" Just go back and work on it. I know I sound trite, but remember, it is the journey that is of value. When you go backward, you have a chance to not just regain the skill you seem to have lost, but also to refine it and make it better. Doing the basics with excellence is everything, so use the time.

When you hit a plateau in your riding, sometimes you might decide to take a step backwards and other times you should shift to simply focus on something different. Again, your trainer is your partner in this journey, and they will have seen it all before and have ideas. My main point is to know that these setbacks and stalls are just part of it. Many of my horse friends have husbands who play golf, and this is a great shared topic. You never get golf "right," or you're never done improving, anyway. And you have setbacks and plateaus. These are deeply mental games, and so the psychological tools and tactics are what wins the day in the end.

Working with Authority Figures and Receiving Feedback in Public during Lessons

If you compete in any sport, you are on display. People see your wins, struggles, and losses. In the horse world, there is something unique about receiving individual feedback in public anytime you are taking a lesson. Even if you are taking a private lesson, there can always be someone around watching. And for us adult newcomers in group lessons, receiving feedback alongside kids thirty years our junior can be humbling.

There is a unique power dynamic when you are an adult, accomplished in most areas of your adult life, taking a horseback riding lesson from a professional. The challenge is to recognize and honor the fact that you are a "baby" rider, while not losing your power and agency as an adult. You will have to be told certain things over and over, because you can only process and retain so many things at once. You're in that path starting at unconscious-incompetence and want to add more and more skills up the ladder to eventually the unconscious-competence category. And if you're active in helping your child in this process, you can coach them through these realities as well.

There are some trainers out there that seem to love having the power over adults, especially accomplished ones. They consider it part of their grooming process to infantilize you and get you to do whatever they tell you in all things related to horses; they will eventually hurt both your confidence and your checking account. These types of trainers are rare—at least I hope they are as rare as they have been in my experience—but watch out for them (see the section about your trainer not owning you, starting on page 123).

Being Prepared for a Whole New Level of Stress When You Start to Show

Performing with your horse in front of a lot of people, both friends and strangers, and a judge adds stress. If you have nerves of steel and are generally a fierce athletic competitor, you will probably be better off than most. If you are like me, with limited public competition experience, you may find it very stressful. For years, when coming out of the competition ring, I could barely remember what happened, would have unintentionally ignored my trainer's final words of advice, and could feel my heart rate over 180 bpm (verified periodically with a heart rate monitor).

It is worth reading the section below about sport psychologists for general advice (there are books out there, a couple of which are listed among the items in the Resources section starting on page 260). If you need help beyond what your trainer is providing, you might even engage one of them for a session or two. My simple counsel is:

- Try not to take yourself terribly seriously.
- Focus on trying to get one single thing right when you go in the ring.
- Enjoy it as much as possible.
- Think about the next stride or jump (or barrel!) ahead of you instead of the one you just messed up.
- Know that you are getting better for the long haul even when you have setbacks.

Understanding that Horse Sport Psychologists Exist for Good Reason

Building off that last bit about sport psychologists being helpful in your riding, someone at one of my barns said when they rode as a child, the barn required all teenage riders to engage a sport psychologist. I love that concept. The barn possibly just wanted help with teenage drama, but I think it's a good idea for any age. As you have the advantage as an adult of knowing yourself, having agency, and having freedom, you should also know enough to ask for help when you can use it.

Each of the prior sections helps explain why I am such a fan of sport psychologists; they are, in short, a secret weapon for this sport, whether you want to compete or not. You may never hire one, which is clearly okay, but almost everyone could benefit at one point or another from a horse sport psychologist with experience in your chosen discipline of the horse world.

Do make sure you understand the qualifications of anyone you engage in this arena. They may not be a credentialed psychologist (however that is regulated in your geography), let alone psychiatrist, but they should be able to explain their background and related training as well as provide references from other riders.

The best approach is frequently to ask around for who has had a good experience with one of these professionals. When you hear the same name from different people, you are likely on a good path.

Be a Forever Student

When it comes to horsemanship and riding, everyone can learn something every day. The best riders in the world are constantly looking for new knowledge, techniques, and tools to refine their craft. Those of us who want to be great horse advocates focus heavily on the latest in horse health and exercise. Those of us who want to perform better with our equine athlete partner work hard to find ways to improve our riding. Think of this path with horses as a forever journey in which you get to learn and grow, and to continually do better with and for your horse.

Read Anything on the Topic of Riding and Horsemanship You Find Appealing

The book in your hand is designed to help you prepare to join the magnificent and slightly crazy horse world. It is not a book specifically about horsemanship or riding. There are so many qualified masters who have written on the topic, and you should look to them. I mention this in the section on page 225 about bonding with your horse: explore the Resources section starting in page 260 and find whatever else you can to fill your reading (or watching or listening) time. Ask anyone you know in the horse world about their favorite people, books, podcasts, or even influencers. There are massive numbers of people posting quality content on Instagram; just get a good list of people there and follow the flow—and avoid, as best you can, the ones who only want to sell you something.

Though it is included in that Resources section, I will call out one book here on this topic. Denny Emerson wrote a book called *Know Better to Do Better*, which focuses on knowledge and a continual desire to learn and grow. I do not know Mr. Emerson, but admire his work, books, and fabulous commentary on his Tamarack Hill Farm Facebook page. Where I count myself as a newcomer at twenty-five years, I count Mr. Emerson as a class legend of the sport at his seventy-years-plus. Nothing in this book of mine teaches you how to ride, but Mr. Emerson's does—as do many of the others in my reference list in the Resources section starting on page 260.

Insist You Start with the Basics

As much as your trainer wants to start with proper basics, you should happily comply. Getting the foundational elements of your horsemanship and riding right will pay dividends later. It is not a straight line of development and at times you will need to backtrack to refine something (see the section starting on page 45 on this forward-and-back journey). However, there are long-term benefits to focusing diligently on your seat, balance, fitness, and connection with your horse, rather than begging to try more advanced things too early. Even if your perfect horse will pack you around to "do" those advanced things, make sure you are getting the feel for it and are not (always) just along for the ride.

STORY

A Good Trainer Finds You the Right Horse for Each Step

In my time in the dressage world, I have been humbled by how much I still needed to learn about my horse's body and my ability to help him work in a way that helps him both feel and perform better. But my short story here is about an insightful trainer who quipped one time that one of her perfect school horses was useless at teaching riders how to produce a square stop (that is, all four feet in perfect alignment). That lovely creature was incapable of stopping any other way than square, and so even a complete newcomer could stop in fine position. It simply meant that other horses—those less inclined to stop perfectly—needed to be engaged to instruct those of us with no idea how to request, let alone produce, a lovely halt.

The section starting on page 260 lists several books which may be helpful for you as you set your priorities and work with your trainer on a lesson and development plan. As you develop in your riding, another way to make sure you are getting solid basics is to go to a clinic with a different trainer or have someone watch your videos for you. It is not that your trainer is not qualified; it is just human nature that they may have tried to correct certain things and eventually moved on with what was "good enough," given how you were responding at the time. About twenty years into my riding, I went back to basics for a few months to fix some balance and position issues I had developed over the years. It was humbling to have my horse on a lead line and me struggling to do some of the exercises as instructed by my amazing new coach, but my riding and relationship with my horse were all the better for it.

Take Lessons Seriously

We are all busy people—even, and perhaps especially, your child-rider, for those of you who are the supporting parent reading this book. It is easy to rock up to your lesson barely on time and without a thought as to what today's instruction might entail. Your trainer will likely take care of you with a plan, some reminders from last time, and continued coaching to the best of their abilities. However, you can get so much more value from each lesson, and training as a whole, if you simply take it more seriously. Here are some simple suggestions:

- **Remind yourself of your objectives.** This step is to remind yourself, and also to help your trainer. If you told your trainer three months prior that your goal was to compete at a certain level, they are still operating on that assumption. If you've changed your mind, you need to let them know; but if not, remember that is the context in which you are taking your lesson today.
- **Reflect on what you want to improve from your last lesson/show/ride.** Hopefully you have in your mind something that needs to be addressed.

If there is nothing compelling from your last lesson or ride, watch a video of yourself and pick on something. But bring that up and see if it is something you can work on that day.

- **Get yourself in the right frame of mind.** Do the breath work suggested on page 18. Then contemplate if you are ready for a lesson. If life is overwhelming right now, it is okay to take a pass when that is the kindest thing for you and your horse. Enjoy a hand graze with him instead.
- **Pay attention throughout.** Listen, reflect, and respond...to everything. That is, to your horse, your trainer, your body, and what you felt when you tried an exercise the previous times. If your trainer was happy with an exercise, but you didn't feel it was your best, ask them to articulate what was great about it and maybe do it again to embed the feeling and the feedback together.
- **Summarize what you learned.** With input from your trainer, reflect on what you learned. Write it down if you have the energy for it; it really helps. A good friend of mine who is a coach for showjumpers always says to start by asking, "What was great?" Even if you made some mistakes, most of it was probably pretty great. Keeping a journal about your horse time is a valuable practice...write down the great stuff first!

Have a Plan When You're Riding on Your Own

Lessons are vital to your horsemanship and riding abilities, especially when you are a true beginner. In fact, you will likely only be able to work with horses and ride when taking a lesson for some time into your riding career. However, as soon as you are given the go-ahead to ride on your own, think about your plan for this time with just you and your horse, whether that means a lesson horse or your own horse. You can just wander around and generally enjoy yourself, or you can take it seriously and practice whatever you are currently learning.

Here are a few recommendations for those who are very new to the sport:

- **Get your tack checked.** Even if the professionals at your barn think you can be trusted to ride outside of a lesson, you should have someone make sure you have groomed and tacked up your horse properly. We all forget things, and sometimes even put things on backwards. There is no shame in asking for help, and not having someone point out a problem could be dangerous (for example, if the girth is loose).
- **Stay in the vicinity of someone.** I usually call this the "someone nearby to call 911 if needed" rule. It's honestly a good rule for everybody to follow, but especially so when you are very new to riding: it is best not to go off by yourself. This includes trail riding. If you want to go for a lovely trail ride, only do so with permission to ensure everyone agrees your horse is suited for such an adventure and you are capable, and with at least one other horse and rider—with one or both of you having a mobile phone securely on your person.

And then a few more recommendations beyond those very early days:

- **Use your lesson notes to guide your ride.** Look back at your notes (whether they are in your head or on paper, see the section above about taking lessons seriously) from your last couple lessons and decide what you think you can work on by yourself.
- **Follow your plan and avoid distractions.** A plan is only helpful if you actually follow it (that whole "execution" thing? It matters). Stick with your plan as best you can, and yet if you are failing hard at something, sometimes it's best to let it go rather than let it get worse and worse. And chats with other riders can be nice, but save those for planned breaks rather than when they happen to show up in the ring.
- **Even for a casual hack, maintain discipline.** My goal in this section is not to make it all sound so serious that you can't just go for a wander with your horse. Sometimes simply bonding with your horse is all you want, and that

is a beautiful thing. The only thing I will add is that you still need to make sure you're not untraining your horse. So, if your horse has a bad habit (especially a dangerous one), a casual ride is not the time when it's okay to let him restart the habit.

- **Share what happened with your trainer.** You don't need to drag them through everything, but if you had particularly good or bad things happen, share them with your trainer. If they have feedback for you (which may include, "Try ABC on your own, but not XYZ"), that is all helpful. You can do this when you show up early for your next lesson, or even through a text if it is brief.

Part of progressing your riding is developing your own assessment of things—not having someone else constantly telling you what to do. You'll learn to teach yourself a bit, or at least catch yourself with your obvious bad habits (the things your trainer corrects at least a half dozen times during each lesson). I believe in the early days of riding you can only think about one thing at a time. And since nothing is really in your muscle memory yet, you're flying a bit blind. However, you can certainly pick one thing—keeping your hands steady in the position your trainer told you, or your legs in the position your trainer told you—and focus on that the entire time you are on your own. And soon enough, some good habits will show up without your having to think about them (and here we come, "unconscious-competence"!).

Get the Most Out of Showing (If You Decide Showing Is for You)

There is an added complexity to this whole journey should you consider showing. If you have no interest, that is of course a fine decision. If you do have an interest in showing, that is also a fine decision, and yet it is best to think it through a bit before jumping into the fray. Hopefully your barn will have a show of sorts on the property or nearby that could count as a practice show before you jump into a big away show. Even when you are used to your trainer evaluating and commenting on your performance in every lesson, there is something different about walking into a ring and being critiqued by a judge you don't know. And the warm-up ring can be even harder to navigate than the actual show ring.

As introduced in the section starting on page 35, being clear about your objectives is fundamental. You may simply want an independent "test" of your abilities to give you further insight on what improvements you can make with your horsemanship and riding. Or you may want to do whatever it takes to get blue ribbons. Just think it through and then talk with your trainer about it. Your trainer should also manage your expectations on the blue-ribbon thing; depending on who you will be competing against (how many competitors, the level of the other riders compared to you, the fanciness of the horses compared to yours, and so on), you may or may not have a viable shot.

Along with your objectives, you need to be honest with yourself and your trainer about your constraints (in terms of time, energy, passion, and money) for showing. If you work weekends, some shows will be out of reach for you. If you work during the week and the only classes for your newbie status are on Wednesdays and Thursdays, you will also struggle. You also need to be prepared for most shows to run on a less-than-predictable schedule. It is unlikely you will be able to show up for just an hour and have your class fit that time perfectly; quite often you need open-ended time. Being clear about your budget for showing is also helpful. Calculate the expected costs up front (see Chapter 3 starting on page 47 for help with that) and then monitor how everything went relative to that budget.

Chapter Nine

Special Notes for Different Roles in the Horse World

There Are Endless Roles in the Horse World, and All of Them Need Their Own Book

This book is for adults who want to join the horse world, either as a horseperson and rider or as a parent to a junior horseperson and rider. Given the breadth of topics covered here, however, it also provides a foundation for the many roles available in the horse world. And so in this final chapter, I provide some advice for a few different roles.

You get to decide how you want to engage with horses and in the horse world. And you will likely shift priorities over time, whether by shifting disciplines, deciding to show, quitting showing, riding less, owning a horse, taking a break from owning a horse, or something else. Over the years I have expanded into owning horses that somebody else rides; I have found it incredibly rewarding, and yes, I know it is an extraordinary privilege to be able to do so. A good friend of mine just switched from hunters to dressage and is so excited about the shift. Another friend has reached an age where she doesn't want to ride, but volunteers weekly to help at a therapeutic riding program. A younger friend of mine is beginning her journey to be a professional in the horse world. Another friend is at the top of the profession as a groom and loves it, even though it can be a difficult life in many ways.

As noted in the beginning, I hope for you that you find a life with horses that feeds your soul and helps you be a better human. Any of the innumerable roles in the horse world can do that for you; it's just a matter of finding the best match for you at this point in your life.

You're an Adult Starting Your Journey with Horses

Given my personal experience starting to ride at thirty, after just a few weeks of riding as a kid, this entire book is for you. That said, there are a few things I would like to emphasize that are unique to being an adult when you start to ride and be around horses. I've organized this to align with the sections in the book that I think are hugely relevant; perhaps it will help you prioritize where you go for more detail.

Key Message	Additional Comments
You're an adult. Own your power, use your skills, and don't let the horse world writ large (or your trainer) infantilize you.	• Sure, you're a baby horseperson, but you're also an adult with agency. • When you are accomplished in other parts of your life, use that experience to help you grow into your role rather than staying small and controlled by the experts.
Horses come first. Take care of your horse, work on your horsemanship and riding, and ignore the barn/show gossip and drama.	• Use all your adult capacity to own your responsibility to do right by the horse(s) in your life. • Barn/show gossip sucks up time and energy; avoid it wherever possible.
Take care of yourself. Be conscious of how you take care of yourself physically and emotionally, and enjoy all that the journey will teach you.	• The more you are in shape, the easier the physical journey. • Get ready to make mistakes in public, and get over it…you are not doing anything wrong; you are simply a beginner. • Be prepared to be annoyed with kids who do not appreciate their horses or their privilege, especially if you didn't have those opportunities as a kid and wanted them.
Face financial realities. Be honest with yourself about your finances, and don't let anyone guilt or peer-pressure you into spending beyond what matches your value system and priorities.	• Everything will cost more than you might guess, and surprise expenses show up all the time; you can do a lot to be proactive and save money, but you can't always count on that to keep you afloat.

Key Message	Additional Comments
Face the realities of limited time. Horses will take as much of your life as you can muster, but there is also a certain minimum…make sure you and those you love can afford your "barn time."	• Carving time out for horses helps with stress (it can be rejuvenating!), and yet you need to make sure it doesn't add stress by overloading you further. Think in advance about what gets cut out so you can add horses into your life. • Across your family, your job, and your friends… some or all of the people in your life will feel the brunt of your absence; make sure you are comfortable with this.
Enjoy every bit of this journey. Have a curious and positive attitude, learn from (rather than beat yourself up for) your mistakes, and maintain a sense of humor.	• Let it all wash over you…horses are magical and will feed your soul. • Don't wish away the early days; indeed, revel in every step of the journey.

You're a Non-Horsey Parent to a Horse-Mad Child

Being new to the horse world as a parent is a unique challenge. You might not even understand why your child is so crazy about horses, but you can see it in their eyes and you want to do what you can to support their riding dreams. So you're reading this book to help understand the why, and also to get prepared to deal with the foreign language of the horse world. Everything in this book applies to you as you think about your child; but rather than being the rider, you are the champion, sponsor, caretaker, and protector of your child in this endeavor.

Key Message	Additional Comments
You're facilitating a learning opportunity. The journey with horses is an extraordinary opportunity for your child to learn discipline, grit, competition, animal care, how to engage with authority figures, and so much more.	• Be clear on the boundaries for the trainer with your child (for example, the trainer is in charge when it comes to safety and coaching; discuss when your presence is required, and when they should come to you for counsel).
Teach animal advocacy. As the adult, it is your job to ensure your child understands their animal care and treatment responsibilities.	• Establish ground rules for what behavior is acceptable relative to horse care (grooming, handling, riding, use of riding aids). • Hold the line: any signs of animal neglect or mistreatment will lead to revocation of the privilege of being with the horse (alone, or at all, depending on what happened).
Safety is job one. This is obvious, but be prepared with the right safety equipment and make sure the entire barn environment supports safe behavior relevant to your child's age.	• Read the section starting on page 30 regarding physical safety precautions necessary in the horse world. • Have frequent discussions with the trainer regarding safety, and if anything happens to anyone in the barn, make sure there is a review of what could be done to avoid such a thing next time. Horse people tend to hate "after action reviews," but make them do it.
Take SafeSport training. Get to know and use the assets offered by the agency in your geography (SafeSport in the US) that provides training and governance for safety for minors in horse sport.	• Read the section starting on page 232 regarding minor safety in the horse world, for your child and for all minors in your midst. • Take all the training that is offered on the topic and be a visible advocate for supporting the safety of everyone in the horse world.

Key Message	Additional Comments
Consider your other kids. This is a bit of a hard one to get right, but you have to know that spending a ton of time and money for one child to ride horses will not go unnoticed by their siblings.	• Decide what you (and your significant other if applicable) think is both equitable and defensible for your approach to supporting one (or more) child riding. • Be clear and consistent with all your children to avoid potential resentment relative to priorities, time, energy, passion, and money.

STORY

A Child Should Earn the Honor of Having a Horse in Their Life

It is a small minority of people who have both the opportunity and means to have horses in their lives. As someone who did not have either growing up, I am perhaps overly aware of the great privilege some young people have to grow up with these creatures. And I struggle when they do not appear to appreciate it.

I have seen snotty juniors not give their horse the love he deserves and get mad at only him when things don't go to plan. Teenage hormones are, of course, a thing, but when a young rider focuses her ire and attitude about something not going well at her four-legged partner, the horse is left reeling. There is no excuse for such behavior.

My opinion—for what it is worth from my arguably easier position as a non-parent—is that parents should draw a line at ethical treatment of the animal. That is, the child should not have the privilege of being around or having a horse if they cannot honor that creature in line with the rights and responsibilities described starting on page 19. They may or may not earn any of the money needed to be part of the horse world, but they can certainly be expected to demonstrate their commitment with responsible, respectful, and reverent behavior towards the horses in their sphere.

You Have Limited Money, and Want to Join the Horse World Economically

Throughout this book I have highlighted ways to avoid spending money, or to spend as economically as you can at varied junctures. I have also been clear that in the early days of your relationship with horses—well before, for example, having your own horse—it is best to not take on too much. Do not lease or buy a horse until you know you can handle it. Engaging with horses prompts many necessary, and an infinite number of optional, ways to spend money. Hopefully the framework below helps you embark cautiously and judiciously.

Key Message	Additional Comments
Start slow. You can be around horses for very little money. Start there and evolve rather than jumping into the deep end.	• Volunteer at a charitable organization (for example, therapeutic riding center) or your local barn (mucking stalls, cleaning the barn, and eventually handling horses when you are competent to do so).
Hold off leasing or buying. The game changes when you are responsible for a horse. Hold off as long as you can—or forever, if that suits you best.	• Take as many lessons per month as you can afford, and then go from there. Show up early and stay late for these lessons…soak up all the barn time you can for the same money. • Do your math before you go any further.
Borrow and bargain shop. For all the gear you need in the horse world, borrow what you can and otherwise look for reasonable sources.	• Talk with your new horse friends and your barn to figure out what you might be able to borrow. • Research local (and online) consignment shops and get help from horse friends to only get what you need. It is so easy to find things you want, but don't really need, in every shop.

Key Message	Additional Comments
Make sure you can afford to show. Showing costs add up quickly; make sure you understand it all before you commit to a show.	• Review local showing opportunities first. Don't spend too much on showing until you know you like it. • Review the full costs with your barn to make sure you know all the bills that will be coming to you. • Make sure you have enough for all your other horse bills before you spend this money.

You Have Plenty of Money, and Do Not Want to Be Swindled

Much of this book tries to keep the focus on the positive people in the horse world who are working hard to make ends meet and do not have calculated plans to steal from you. However, as noted in the sections starting on pages 57 and 169, there are those in the horse world who do not treat you or your money respectfully, by either wasting it unnecessarily or taking more than they deserve. I absolutely want anyone working in the horse industry to be able to make a decent living. But I abhor usury rates and hidden fees that are charged because either a) they feel they deserve it and can get away with it because you have so much money, or b) they can't manage their business well and are regularly out of money.

Find Equine-Specific Experts to Help You in This Journey

For those of you with a massive amount of money (let's call you uber-wealthy), my counsel is to get an advisor in the horse world beyond your trainer. There is too much potential for a conflict of interest between you and the trainer, and it is better to keep things professional and transparent from the beginning. You may already have a family office or a financial manager who runs your shop; they could likely perform this same function in the horse world with just a bit of support from professionals with experience in equine law, business, financials, deals, and management.

If you don't have the right kind of person or team with capacity, you might engage what I like to call an "equine consigliere" to manage this all for you as an integral part of your family office or support team. Your trainer may balk at having another layer of control, but it will make everything easier and safer for you... and you are the one paying the bills. A great trainer will see the positive potential to keep things aboveboard, including bills being paid on time without them having to chase your busy self.

If you are simply wealthy (not uber-wealthy), you might not want to have a dedicated support professional, but you could hire a part-time equine consigliere or manage the team of equine-related professionals yourself. Regardless of the amount of money you have, you should be very clear on your budget and send continual signals that you are holding to that number. These signals can be as simple as reading every bill in detail and asking for receipts when you have questions (you or a financial support person can do this), finding better deals for anything on the list to be purchased (you might task your horse-mad child with this exercise, regardless of your level of funds), and saying no when offered a more expensive option for anything (whether that be a horse or a bridle).

A Well-Organized Support Team Can Also Help with
Horse Care Management

The other function of equine professionals supporting you, whether all roles are wrapped up in an equine consigliere or spread out across the individual professionals in each field, is helping to take the best care of your horses. The horse world is not the best with records—even with a few startups trying diligently to improve the technology available, it remains quite a desert for helpful tools—and so having rigorous record-keeping and tracking can keep you ahead on not just finances, but health care as well. Remember the Horse Care Plan,

Horse Care Tracker, and Horse Exercise Tracker templates on pages 218, 221, and 223 respectively; these are simple templates that can be expanded to be as sophisticated as you like and can afford.

You Want to Help Improve the Diversity of the Horse World

There are magnificent examples of diversity in the horse world. Indeed, there are very few sports with such a blend of age, gender, and sexual orientation. The horse world also has unique possibilities for people with disabilities; these include not just competitive options up to and including the Olympics, but also options for people not interested in horses *per se* but in the therapeutic benefits of working with and potentially riding them.

And yet also, and not uniquely, the horse world struggles massively with diversity in terms of both a) socio-economic status, and b) race and ethnicity. The former is a bit obvious given all that you now understand about how expensive horses can become; it also seems to only be getting worse on that front, especially if you want any chance at being competitive at the highest levels. The latter is not simply due to the former, as some would like to believe, but is also grounded in innumerable factors, not least of which is it can be a very non-welcoming sport to people of color.

When I started consulting in 1990, fresh out of undergrad, we were just starting to take diversity seriously. After decades of working on various programs—we did make progress, but not enough—I finally decided that I was no longer willing to sit in a room with a bunch of women talking about the "women problem." I told my leadership peers, "I will mentor women and I will champion women, but I'm not going to waste my time on non-market-facing activities because a) that is time away from the truly valued task of me doing a brilliant job or selling and delivering more quality work, and, to put a fine point on it, b) women are not the problem." (There was an expletive in that last quote—you can guess where.) The same applies here. It is not the job of people of color to figure out how to make the system better. It is the system's job to decide if it cares about the problem and then do something about it.

There are good people out there trying to make this sport more welcoming. It is my humble hope that this book is helpful to people who don't feel naturally welcome in the horse world, and encourages them to, if they want to, give it a try.

You Want to Help Horse Welfare in the World

This area is an endless opportunity to do good by horses anywhere in the world. There are innumerable charities, so many that I will not endeavor to include a list here. But think about all the various forms of equine-related charities, some of which have volunteering opportunities:

- General horse welfare (non-profit organizations focused on horse welfare through direct support, public education, legislative advocacy, horse sport rules and regulations, and more).
- Wild horse support (varying breeds and numbers by country).
- Working horse support (global endeavor to improve the conditions and lives of working horses).
- Rescue and rehabilitation (some breed-specific, and others general, with the objective for the horses to go back to private ownership and care).
- Rescue and retirement (similar to the previous category, but the horses remain at what is frequently called a sanctuary).
- Equine-assisted therapies (horses helping with physical, mental, and emotional challenges and disabilities).

Epilogue

After 75,000 words about how to do right by horses, and a bit on taking care of yourself, I want to end with something that came to me only recently. It will be obvious on its face, but perhaps it's just with age that I finally understand it. And that is: make every effort to give yourself as much grace as you show to these beautiful horses. Because you deserve it as well.

To bring this to life, I share below something I wrote in the middle of the night when I was visiting the very spiritual place of Machu Picchu in Peru. I had been contemplating why the horse Machu (discussed on page 13) means so much to me. And, indeed, why I have tears in my eyes almost anytime I think or talk about him, let alone when I still get to kiss his retired nose.

I then reflected on all that I strive to do and be for Machu (even when mostly by proxy, not being his day-to-day carer), and all my horses, and contemplated that perhaps I could do and be the same for myself.

I hope this lands for you in some way. It helped me further absorb how much horses have taught me about being human.

November 2022, an unedited midnight scribble…my feelings and actions about the exquisite horse, Machu. That is, "I _____ Machu," and perhaps, in some cases, "I _____ Me."

1. Love
2. Fight for
3. Take care of
4. Watch out for
5. Celebrate
6. Applaud
7. Monitor the health of
8. Touch lovingly
9. Am amazed by
10. Reward
11. Coddle
12. Check on

13. Protect
14. Clothe
15. Properly shoe :-)
16. Groom
17. Bask in the greatness of
18. Share with others
19. Look over head to toe
20. Buy the best medical care
21. Buy the best bodyworker care
22. Laugh with
23. Feed only the best food to
24. Track nutrition for
25. Pay attention to moods of
26. Pay attention to niggles of
27. Cry for when in pain or discomfort
28. Champion
29. Revere
30. Admire
31. Take precautions for the safety of
32. Am besotted with
33. Ensure gets good exercise
34. Ensure not overworked
35. Defend body and reputation
36. Photograph and video
37. Learn from
38. Am humbled by
39. Know is both very special and one of many
40. Lose sleep over (at times)
41. Am 100% confident in
42. Never question (integrity)
43. Spend time with (quiet and otherwise)
44. Cherish, full stop, and time with
45. Am lucky to be with and around
46. Triple check best care for
47. Give treats to
48. Show up in the hard times for
49. Have unwavering and unconditional love for
50. Am here forever, and to the end for

Resources

These are books that I recommend, both to supplement the information in this book and grow your interest in horses and equestrian sport, listed in no particular order. More books and other recommendations can be found in the Resources section of my website (AndreaSinner.com).

Centered Riding | Sally Swift

How Good Riders Get Good: Daily Choices that Lead to Success in Any Equestrian Sport | Denny Emerson

Begin and Begin Again: The Bright Optimism of Reinventing Life with Horses | Denny Emerson

Seabiscuit: An American Legend | Laura Hillenbrand

The Tao of Equus: A Woman's Journey of Healing and Transformation through the Way of the Horse | Linda Kohanov

Wild Horses of Skydog: Blue Zeus & Families | Clare Staples

The United States Pony Club Manual of Horsemanship | Three Manuals: Basic for Beginners D Level, Intermediate for Horsemanship C1-C2 Level, and AdvancedHorsemanship HB-A Levels | Susan E. Harris & United States Pony Club

The Man Who Listens to Horses: The Story of a Real-Life Horse Whisperer | Monty Roberts

Horses Never Lie: The Heart of Passive Leadership | Mark Rashid

Whole Heart, Whole Horse: Building Trust Between Horse and Rider | Mark Rashid

Anne Kursinski's Riding and Jumping Clinic: A Step-by-Step Course for Winning in the Hunter and Jumper Rings | Anne Kursinski

Dressage Between the Jumps: The Secret to Improving Your Horse's Performance Over Fences | Jane Savoie

Dressage 101: The Ultimate Source of Dressage Basics in a Language You Can Understand | Jane Savoie

That Winning Feeling! Program Your Mind for Peak Performance | Jane Savoie

The Dressage Rider's Journal: Planner & Calendar Dressage Rider Organizer | Ruth Hogan-Poulsen

The Original Horse Bible: The Definitive Source for All Things Horse | Moira C. Reeve and Sharon Biggs

Improving Equine Mobility: Illustrated Applications of Fascial Informed Techniques | Wendy Coren, D.C.

The Concussion Repair Manual: A Practical Guide to Recovering from Traumatic Brain Injuries | Dr. Dan Engle

Equine Law and Horse Sense | Julie I. Fershtman

Ride Big: The Ultimate Guide to Building Equestrian Confidence | John Haime

Horse Brain, Human Brain: The Neuroscience of Horsemanship | Janet L. Jones, PhD

Horse Speak: Conversations with Horses in Their Language | Sharon Wilsie and Gretchen Vogel

The Art of Horsemanship | Xenophon

Index